THE **PRIVATE PRACTICE**
Survival Guide

THE PRIVATE PRACTICE

Survival Guide

A Journey to Unlock Your Freedom to Success

BRANDON SEIGEL

The Private Practice Survival Guide
A Journey To Unlock Your Freedom To Success

Copyright ©2019 by Brandon Seigel
All rights reserved.

Published by Rebel Press
Austin, TX
www.RebelPress.com

ISBN: 978-1-64339-937-9
Library of Congress: 2018960840

Printed in the United States of America

Table of Contents

THE PRIVATE PRACTICE
Survival Guide

ACKNOWLEDGEMENTS

In the words of Douglas Adams, "I may not have gone where I intended to go, but I think I have ended up where I intended to be." Throughout my childhood, my grandmother, Norma Seigel, would ask me frequently: "Brandon, what do you want to be when you grow up?" She always hoped I would be a doctor or a lawyer. The reality is this question has haunted me for a better part of my life. Although I did not always know my exact professional journey, I know now I ended up in the right place. I love coaching people and inspiring business professions to uncover their goals and succeed at them.

This book would not be possible without the encouragement of my parents. My mother always tells me I have an unstoppable passion for helping others be productive, and my father continually inspires me with his enthusiasm for writing, teaching, and motivating audiences.

The Private Practice Survival Guide is dedicated to and in honor of my grandfathers, David Seigel and Melvin Spellens.

I always say we need to honor the past, present, and future as that is what makes us who we are and who we want to be. With that being said, I am the man who I am today because of the following people: David and Norma Seigel, Melvin and Charlotte Spellens, Gary and Randi Seigel (greatest parents a kid could dream of), Eli & Fredlyn Berger (the greatest in-laws and partners in our private practice journey), Matthew and Allison Seigel, Jordan and Natsuki

1

Seigel, and Benjamin and Jamie Berger.

I save the best for last! I wake up every morning with vigor for life because of the love of my life and truly the person who makes me the best me, day in and day out—my loving wife, Tamara Seigel. Thank you for believing in me and your constant sacrifice helping me reach my highest aspirations! As for the future, my ambition to create a greater world is because of my amazing children, Sophia and Jonah! Last shout out must be to my best friend, Chester the Golden Retriever.

INTRODUCTION

Over the past fifteen years, I have had the privilege to support private practice entrepreneurs throughout the country while also embarking on my own entrepreneurial ventures. I was born into a family of professors, entrepreneurs, and authors—and I married into a family of occupational therapists. It is with great passion that I created this book with the goal of empowering entrepreneurs throughout the world who have a vision or dream about creating change within our society through service-oriented business models.

Throughout my experience, I have fallen many times and been fortunate to have been picked up through mentorship, life lessons, and establishing new skill sets. When preparing this book, it truly poured out of me, but it took a long time for me to formulate the title. It was not until I reflected on all my stories that I realized that this manuscript represents my very own *Private Practice Survival Guide*. The very words in this book and lessons that I share have brought me and those around me the success that we all celebrate.

The purpose of this *Private Practice Survival Guide* is to provide you with the very same mentorship, essential learning lessons, and new skill sets to help you create the success you have always yearned for, while preventing the scars that occurred during my journey. I recommend that you read this guide once through without writing a single note and just take in based on the core messages that resonate most with you. Then go through the table of contents and identify each chapter that represents a fear or weakness that you have identified. Please go through those chapters that you have identified, re-read them, and write down the following for each one:

1. Why did I feel inclined to read this chapter again?

2. What are three takeaways that I received from re-reading this chapter?

3. How can I implement three things from this chapter in the next 90 days?

This book is a journey. Not every chapter may represent your journey, but there are stories and messages that can transform the trajectory of your private practice goals!

Enjoy, share, and implement! We are on this journey together.

CHAPTER 1

The Risk Factor: Identifying the Private Practice Entrepreneur within You

> *"When you grow up you tend to get told that the world is the way it is and your life is just to live your life inside the world. Try not to bash into the walls too much. Try to have a nice family life, have fun, save a little money.*
>
> *That's a very limited life. Life can be much broader once you discover one simple fact: Everything around you that you call life was made up by people that were no smarter than you. And you can change it, you can influence it... Once you learn that, you'll never be the same again."*
> —Steve Jobs

We all have our own personal definition of what true wealth is. It might involve money or time or simply the freedom to do what you wish. The same standard you hold for your own success won't be true of the next person.

There's a classic story that comes to mind about a fisherman and an entrepreneur, often attributed to Brazilian writer Paulo Coelho.

A businessman from America goes on vacation in Mexico to a tiny village by the ocean. The village has a single boat with one fisherman. The businessman is an investment banker, always on the lookout for a promising market opportunity. He compliments the fisherman on the quality of the fish he's caught that day. But he notices that the fisherman has already called it a day—and it's still fairly early in the afternoon.

He asks the fisherman, "Why don't you stay out longer? You can catch some more fish and make more money for your family."

The fisherman replies that he has caught enough for the day. His family has their needs satisfied—they have their next meal.

The businessman replies, "Well, what do you do with the rest of your time?"

"I sleep late...I do some fishing. I play with my children and take siestas with my wife. I go down into the village each evening. I sip wine and play guitar with my amigos."

The businessman scoffs a bit at this. He tells the fisherman that he holds an MBA and can help him to get his business to scale. He tells him that if he would put more time into fishing, he could buy a bigger boat...then another boat...and soon he would have a whole fleet of fishing boats. Instead of going out and fishing himself, he could hire others to do all the fishing for him. Instead of selling his catch to a middleman, he could open his own cannery—controlling the product and the processing and distribution.

Of course, he would need to leave this village to really be a global player—he would have to move to Mexico City, or even Los Angeles. But in 15-20 years, he would be wildly rich beyond his greatest dreams.

The fisherman asked, "But then what?"

"Well," the American replied, "you could retire. Then you could move to a small coastal village and relax. You could sleep late, fish a little bit, spend time with your family, relax in the village in the evenings, sip wine with your friends..."

• • • • •

The fisherman may have lacked formal education or business training, but he did have an insight that many of us miss, the businessman included—success is subjective.

For some of us, it means climbing the corporate ladder; for some of us, our goal is to take it easy and carve out more time for our families. There is no single answer for any of us—and no sense in spending your life pursuing someone else's dreams.

I share this story because each of you has a vision of what your goals are. You may already be living your dream but don't recognize it.

My clients work in a wide variety of areas—ranging from occupational and speech therapists to registered dietitians, social workers, family therapists, and everyone in between.

Though they come from different training and educational backgrounds, their common link is their goal: they are passionate about changing the world by creating "artisan-like" health, wellness, and education private practices throughout the United States.

If you're reading this book, you very likely fall into a specific niche of sorts—you are a trained, highly skilled medical professional and you are interested in pursuing opportunities in entrepreneurship. Know your stuff inside and out when it comes to your expertise as a healthcare professional—but you know that you will be flexing new muscles along the way of your journey into business.

My hope is to help you along that journey. I know that it can be easy to feel isolated along the way. I specialize in helping my clients bring their businesses to the next level—building effective operations, streamlining their bottom-line, and scaling profitably.

I help them strategize how to stand out in a crowded marketplace.

My ultimate goal is to empower clinicians, helping them to forge careers as successful entrepreneurs in their own right—and thrive even in the midst of an often challenging business environment.

I know firsthand how challenging it can be. At the age of 25, I became the Vice-President of Operations for a start-up employing more than 250 employees. Over time, I was recognized as a leader in workforce management—and I take special pride in being referred to as an entrepreneur's best friend.

However, it took considerable time to get here. There were many, many challenging days along the way, when I was not at all certain of what the outcome would be. I have learned that experience truly is the best teacher—and my 13 years of experience in executive leadership has allowed me to make an impact, helping other entrepreneurs reach their organizations' goals.

I am concerned at how many small businesses in this space fail each day in America. We are depending on entrepreneurs to inject new ideas and bold action into our bloated healthcare system.

Setting Your Goals

The first step in building this success requires you to take a step back and consider your intentions. It is essential that you define your professional goals, personal goals, and ideal vision for success.

My role as a "private practice coach" is not to influence your "end goal" but to help you reach it through winning strategies, secrets, and new perspectives. It is not my place as "the businessman" to influence you on your "why" or your "what," but rather shed light on the "how."

The businessman visiting that village in Mexico might have had strategies for the fisherman to scale and grow his business. He may have had the best of intentions in sharing his expertise. But what he failed to recognize was that the fisherman was already at his end goal. He had already achieved his own pinnacle of success.

It is essential that you define your vision because you are the one living it day in and day out. As my grandfather used to say, "Brandon, bigger is not always better…it is just a different vision."

The #1 Question Clinicians Don't Like To Answer

Over the last three years, I have had the great pleasure to meet with private practice owners throughout the United States. Through my workshops and private consulting appointments, I have been able to identify a commonality in nearly every private practice entrepreneur that I have met within the health, wellness, and education space. The commonality is that they are driven by purpose, not simply maximizing profits. That is why I specialize in working with entrepreneurs in this given market. I am too inspired, driven, and motivated by purpose.

However, I have also found a commonality in response to my first and most important question that I ask a private practice entrepreneur. Their response to this single most important question is typically a chuckle, followed by a little bit of blush, and then about a thirty-second awkward pause. The question I have just asked them is… "How much money do you want to make?"

It is amazing, but I have found that private practice entrepreneurs in the health, wellness, and education space feel embarrassed and ashamed to admit they want to make money and define their financial goals. We do pick up on cues in our culture that success is equivalent to greed; popular entertainment often offers narratives in which those who pursue money are lacking in meaningful ambition or empathy for their fellow citizens.

I typically follow up during this awkward pause with, "It's okay. I understand that it is a tough question to answer, but should I assume you want to work for free?"

At this point, the private practice entrepreneur is almost starting to question my intentions because of how forthcoming I am with this question. I then make sure to soften the moment. I share with them that I hold the same passion about service-based entrepreneurship. I fully recognize that purpose must be the driving force—otherwise we would likely go into a much less-stressful line of work. However, revenue must be the fuel for this work.

I then add a little bit of laughter to the conversation by saying: "Isn't it a faux pas that society makes the choices that we do about value and compensation? We seem too comfortable with actors like Dwayne Johnson, also known as "The Rock," making over 60 million dollars annually for appearing in blockbusters—but then private practitioners like you who are truly changing the world are slighted for wanting to make the same."

My purpose is not to inspire you to be a millionaire but to empower you to name your financial goals and not be ashamed of those financial goals. I believe that as long as you are ethical, deliver quality, and create real within your domain, then you have every right to name to create real financial goals of any magnitude as it feels right for you.

Please note that the difference between financial magnitudes is in the scalability of your private practice vision. The reason that I insist a private practice entrepreneur name at the very least an introductory financial goal is that we must begin to explore the scalability of their business model.

For example, there is a profound difference in business models between a client telling me they would be thrilled to make their current salary of $70K net as a private practice entrepreneur—and one who shares with me a vision of pulling in $250K net in their first year. I always begin the "vision process" by naming the net financial goals so that the follow-up step is identifying the "how" and "when" which we will cover later on in this chapter.

Are You Pulling Or Directing The Cart?

As you begin to identify your financial goals, your business model will formulate around an essential question. "Are you pulling the cart or are you directing the cart?"

If you are "pulling the cart," so to speak, then you are most likely exploring a sole proprietorship private practice in which you are the sole product, in the form of the services that you offer. There are both benefits and drawbacks to a sole proprietorship business model.

I tend to see this business model as a "1099 Independent Contractor" business model in which you don't rely on others to deliver the service, and ultimately your business model revenue is based 100 percent on your time and delivery methods.

The drawbacks of this business model are that your financial revenue is typically tied to your productivity. In other words, when you go on vacation you are not making money. At the end of the day, "You work for your business" versus "Your business works for you."

The benefit of the "sole proprietorship," on the other hand, is that you have 100 percent control over the service delivery and product and have a very limited overhead and responsibility beyond yourself. If you are a "control addict" and don't enjoy taking on major risks, then I would say this may be a better model for you because the other model we are about to discuss takes a much higher tolerance for risk, a higher degree of trust, and a commitment to workforce empowerment.

If your private practice vision incorporates utilizing other practitioners in your service delivery method, then you most likely fall under my category entitled "directing the cart." In this type of business model, you have a vision for employing other practitioners to contribute to the service delivery. It is not to say that you are not delivering the services as well, but your role under this model is different from a sole proprietorship. In most cases, you would be an employer—responsible for managing others and assuming more of the responsibilities we typically associate with a "boss."

In order to succeed in this framework, you truly must thrive on empowering a team to carry out your private practice delivery vision. This type of business model holds much greater risk and financial responsibility. However, when executed right, it may have a greater reward both from a purpose and financial perspective. The goal of an "employer-based business model" is to build the private practice to a point where it can "work for you" as much as "you work for it."

As an example, you can take a vacation and revenue will come in which gives you a new sense of freedom. The key to unlocking the freedom from success as an "employer-based" private practice is hiring smart and establishing top-level staff, positive cash flow, effective metrics, and efficient administrative systems. These are all areas that we will discuss in-depth in this book.

As illustrated in the "The Fisherman and The Business Man," a businessman's advice is only advice, and it is essential that you identify your private practice vision. Whether you are drawn to "pulling the cart" or "directing the cart," there is no right or wrong but rather different paths to success.

Understanding the Value of Exchange

I have worked hard to be where I am today. However, I also recognize that I was born with some enormous advantages in life that have contributed to my success. I was fortunate to be surrounded by a family with strong entrepreneurial roots dating back multiple generations from both parents' lineage. Both of my grandfathers found great success as entrepreneurs in totally different industries, scalability, and business models. My grandparents were products of the Depression in which they each introduced essential business foundations that have truly changed my life. They set an example of thriftiness, grit, and resilience that continues to resonate with me today.

One of the core life lessons that my grandfathers drilled into me was the value of "exchange."

I find this to easily be one of the most misunderstood notions in today's generation gap. In a time, where millennials are being identified as an "entitled" workforce and employers are focused on competing with who can offer the greatest "work-life balance," society is not acknowledging that exchange comes in all different shapes, sizes, and colors. It is essential not just to evaluate an exchange based on monetary compensation—because it is proven that money does not always equal the largest "ROI." Just ask any newly minted law grad who is miserable at their big firm despite their signing bonus.

When I graduated college, I was truly blessed to be given an opportunity to work for a leading manufacturer of sports and leisure products. I was an eager college graduate, hungry to show off what I could do. There is simply no competing with someone who is willing to work all hours of the day and night, without the distractions of family and responsibility that tend to come with time. I had an ambition that was truly uncontrollable.

As I began to learn the business and find success in my role as an account executive, I had not quite learned that exchange was greater than just a monetary compensation exchange. I had a business idea that I was passionate about implementing for my employer and was given an opportunity to develop it. That business idea ended up being a stepping stone for a new division within the company and brought additional growth to the company.

I remember sitting down with my maternal grandfather, Melvin Spellens, and sharing with him about my recent hard work and the detailed revenue forecast that we put together for this business idea. As I continued to share everything with my grandfather, my story went from excitement and passion to kvetching. I was complaining that I was putting all this time into developing something that I had no monetary exchange for.

My statement was, "They make millions of dollars while I see none of it." Yes, as I look back now, I can admit it—I was suffering from what you might call "M.E.S."...Millennial Entitlement Syndrome.

I will never forget the next moment. The first thing that my

13

grandfather asked me was, "Are you getting paid for your time?"

I followed up with, "Yes, but…"

My grandfather looked me square in the eyes and said, "Brandon, you are getting more than you even know. You are truly blessed with the opportunity that has been presented to you. You are getting paid to learn, grow, and create. There is no greater value that they could be exchanging with you. You must work hard, learn hard, and never forget the hand that is feeding you."

From that moment on, I realized that my grandfather had taught me a life lesson that truly changed my path as a person. After that day, I never looked at an exchange as just a monetary compensation structure again. I realized that exchange could include so much more than dollars and cents—extending to education, mentorship, professional growth, purpose, philanthropy, fun memories and much more.

Financial compensation is but only one form of exchange. It is essential that entrepreneurs in our space identify exchange beyond just financial because otherwise, you burn out. Money is important, but it is likely not enough to sustain you through truly hard work over the long haul. Private practice entrepreneurship is not an easy venture, and I share with all my clients that you can't just get into private practice for the money. I recommend to all my clients to identify all the different exchanges that they are looking for when owning a private practice. The #1 exchange should be connected with "WHY" you're launching a private practice.

Defining Your Why

> *"People don't buy what you do; they buy why you do it."*
> —Simon Sinek

Motivational speaker and marketing consultant Simon Sinek struck a chord with many in his book *Start with Why*, which he parlayed into a viral Ted Talk. Sinek vividly illustrates how great leaders throughout history—ranging from Martin Luther King Jr. to Steve Jobs and the Wright Brothers—approached their message differently than the majority of us. Rather than pitching their followers on what their ideas could do for them, they began with the premise of why it was important. Steve Jobs didn't start with "Buy an Apple computer"—he started with "Apple believes in making beautiful products."

The single most important item that all private practice entrepreneurs must name clearly when exploring their vision is their "why." This is one of the single most contributions to defining your private practice business model, foundation and vision. The business model should be a reflection of the meaning of your vision.

For example, my wonderful mother-in-law, Fredlyn Berger, a licensed occupational therapist, launched her first private practice in 2003. When I asked about her own "why," she was very clear with me. She said she invested a lot of time to fully think this through. She shared that after 30 years of clinical experience working in hospitals, schools, and nursing homes, she wanted to create a company culture that she had never experienced elsewhere. She wanted the experience of a community-based private practice—founded on principles that empowered clinical collaboration, continued educational growth, and integrity.

She elaborated that she also wanted a private practice that provided her freedom one day to take more time off. She wanted to exert more control over her future, rather than being controlled by the whims of others.

It became clear over time that she over-estimated her ability to take time off as she works harder than anyone I know. However, based on her vision statement—on her "Why"—she formulated a business model in which she "directed the cart" and attracted team members that were empowered because of her vision, purpose, and her own "Why."

Is Your Private Practice A Hobby, Charity, Or Business?

The single most common challenge that I find in private practices in today's environment is that private practice entrepreneurs are afraid to run their practice like a "business." They are faced with a fear that it may take away from their "purpose," and also confront the fear that there is an ethical dilemma. They can't seem to allow themselves to fully embrace the idea that they are entrepreneurs.

This could have something to do with negative portrayals in the media of capitalism. I love shows like *Billions* and *Empire* as much as the next person—but our culture is clearly inundated with characters who send the message that pursuing success is tantamount to blind greed. Perhaps some of this is attributed to lingering resentment about Wall Street in the wake of the 2008 financial crisis. Given how purpose-driven many medical professionals are, they are often left with the message that going into business is a grubby affair.

In early 2017, I was helping an occupational therapist by the name of Erica in North Carolina troubleshoot why her private practice was failing. Erica had launched a private practice with an incredible purpose, a true heart of gold, and a burning desire to support the community that she loved so dearly. Erica assembled a truly world-class team of clinicians and assembled a big payer mix because of the needs surrounding this community.

Yet after our initial meeting, I realized that we had a serious problem. Where Erica failed was in putting her purpose before the business planning process. It became clear that she had dug herself into a major cash flow and financial situation. In addition, she had leveraged her home by taking a line of credit and made the ultimate financial sacrifices to launch this private practice.

As we began to build on our conversations, I realized that Erica had a major misunderstanding that ultimately was preventing her success. Erica simply did not know how to run her private practice like a business. She believed that if she gave great service, then all would fall into place on the business side. She put her trust in all of her clients to pay their bills, the insurance companies to pay their bills, and ultimately her faith that everything would just come together perfectly.

When reviewing her financials, I noticed that Erica was getting paid by only about 25 percent of her clients for copays and coinsurance. I asked her about this, and she said that her clients couldn't afford to pay their co-pays, but she felt there was an ethical dilemma in not providing services to them. I bit my tongue at this point because I did not want to come off as the stereotypical ruthless businessman.

I then continued to explore her financials when I noticed that she was only getting paid 70 percent of the time from the health insurance companies. She also had a ton of revenue stuck in her aging report that was over 120 days old. I inquired about this out-point, and she said the billing company was looking into it. I asked when was the last time the billing company had followed up on these cycles, and she said she did not know.

At this point, my cheeks were getting red like the color of my hair because I hate to see great people self-sabotage their survival. The reality is that Erica did not know better. Her heart was in the right place, but she jumped into this without really preparing herself with the necessary business fundamentals and strategies.

I noticed one final troubling aspect of her business—this was truly the straw that broke the camel's back. I noticed in her financials that she was paying her therapists more money per treatment than the contracted rate she was supposed to be paid.

At this point, I dug deep into my gut to try and pull the most controlled calm voice that I could come up with (think James Earl Jones).

I said, "Erika, why are you paying your clinicians more than the contracted rates?"

She looked at me with a little bit of embarrassment and said, "Brandon, these are the best clinicians in the area, and I didn't want to lose them."

I realized I needed to confront Erika and that this may be the most challenging conversation that I had yet. Erika knew her private practice was failing. Thus, she reached out to me. However, I truly don't think she had any reality of how bad her financial situation had become. She continued to pile up debt thinking that everything would fall into place eventually.

I went on to ask Erika an essential question, "Did you create your private practice with the purpose of being a hobby, charity, or business?" She looked at me puzzled, and tears started to fall down her face. I could see that Erika was at a point of panic, so I hugged her and shared that this was not the first time I had seen it.

The reality is that it is all too common. I find stories like this to be a typical occurrence in the private practice community, although she had leveraged more than most to make her private practice vision a reality. I assured her that I was there to help, to be a source of support, and to empower her to be the best private practice entrepreneur she could be, all while staying true to her vision and purpose. I insisted that we could turn it around—but it would take her changing her viewpoint and confronting her priorities.

Borrowing a page from investment legend Warren Buffet, I told her that priority #1 was that she couldn't lose money; priority #2 is that she couldn't lose money, and priority #3 is that she couldn't lose money.

It might sound silly I have to share that, but truly most of the private practitioners that I encounter have a heart of gold. I told Erica that once her private practice was at a place where it was not losing money, then she would have the freedom to decide what she wanted to do with the rest of the revenue—give to charity, invest it into a hobby, or whatever her big picture goal was.

After several months, Erica and I worked hard to create change within her private practice. It was essential to carry out her vision of providing incredible services without losing money. We created a strategy to retain her incredible clinicians while not losing money on the visits. We came up with a game plan for them that had financial bonuses built in which would ultimately bring her private practice to a new level of success. In addition, we fired her billing company and came up with billing and collection strategies that changed the course of her entrepreneurial journey to success.

Although Erika's practice is still a work in progress, I am excited to report that her practice is well on track. Her business generates a positive cash flow every month. It no longer loses revenue. The key was taking responsibility for the business and not feeling ashamed of making business decisions while still staying true to her "why."

Emotional Necessities

Something that entrepreneurs don't always recognize is the role that emotion plays in creating a successful private practice.

In my days as a student at California Lutheran University, I had a memorable professor for my MBA entrepreneurship class. He taught us that there are two emotions that entrepreneurs must tap into on a regular basis when scaling a successful business venture. The two emotions were love and fear.

At first, I was shocked that these were the two emotions that he highlighted. As I look back now, however, with the benefit of hindsight after years of supporting entrepreneurs, I must share that it truly resonates with me. Both of these "feelings" create a vulnerability that is truly a necessity in scaling a successful private practice based around purpose.

"Words may show a man's wit but actions his meaning."
—Benjamin Franklin

Let's start with the one of the most loaded terms in the English language—*love*.

There are so many interpretations of the meaning; some would not define love as an emotion but as an action. I embrace love as an emotion and feeling. Love is often defined "as an intense feeling of deep affection." The fact that love can be an action as well as a feeling is essential when tapping into it as a private practice owner.

I have found in my own experience that love fuels passion and ultimately supports us in working hard to achieve our purpose. I always say that love is the fuel that pushes me to work hard without burning out. It is also the tool that empowers a team and clientele. Your private practice should truly become your labor of love in order for you to stick with it through the inevitable tough times. Therefore, it is essential that you ensure your private practice vision evokes love and that you tap into the emotion of love on a regular basis because that will fuel you through adversity.

Then there is the concept of "*fear*," which most people seem to consider a weakness. I believe fear can be utilized as a strength when embraced in the right way. Fear is defined as "an unpleasant emotion caused by the belief that someone or something is dangerous, likely to cause pain or a threat." I have found that fear is what prepares us to strategize and embrace change.

An example: If you embrace your fear or concern on how the healthcare reform will impact your private practice, then you will most likely research, prepare, and advocate to embrace the change in a way where you can survive and thrive. When someone does not tap into fear or define a threat, it is often a warning sign that they are not adept at evaluating reality. There is a difference between reacting to fear by not doing something and preparing for fear.

Overall, I have found that love is the tool that fuels my work ethic, and fear is the tool that drives me to research, prepare, and strategize as a private practice entrepreneur. My desire for you is to design a love-based business strategy and utilize the fear to anchor you.

Who, What, When, and How!

As you are defining your private practice vision, you will begin to uncover and embrace your "why." It is important to recognize that part of defining your "why" is identifying its relationship to the following key questions: Who is the target demographic? What is your core service or product? When are you looking to start? And how are you going to execute your vision?

I find that entrepreneurs have an easier time defining their why because it can be drawn to purpose and intention. The other questions can pose a challenge because one may wonder how big or small their vision should be. I tend to recommend that you have a short-term vision that you can execute within one year, combined with a five-year vision as well.

Here is an example based on my private practice coaching business model:

My Why: I am concerned that small businesses are failing every day and believe that the "American Dream" of entrepreneurship is the secret to providing better health, wellness, and education services in the United States of America.

My Who: Private Practice Practitioners & Service Providers With A Dream Of Becoming Entrepreneurs: Occupational Therapists, Physical Therapists, Speech Language Pathologists, Eastern Medicine Specialists, Registered Dietitians, Social Workers, Teachers, Marriage, and Family Therapists who are passionate about changing the world by creating "artisan-like" health, wellness, and education private practices throughout the United States.

My What: Private Practice Consultations, Private Practice Entrepreneur Coaching Program, Private Practice Management Services, Private Practice Bootcamp Courses, Private Practice Survival Guide Book, Private Practice Co-Working Spaces.

My When: I launched my new private practice coaching/consulting model on January 1, 2017, with a goal to release my book by December 31, 2018, and ultimately support over 1,000 private practice entrepreneurs by 2022.

My How: I am guest lecturing and a keynote speaker in front of over 500 health and wellness professionals annually. I am writing the *Private Practice Survival Guide* book to spread the vision of changing the world through private practice entrepreneurship. I created a private practice boot camp digital course to support the needs of private practice entrepreneurs throughout the United States. I currently consult to private practice entrepreneurs throughout the United States.

Something to keep in mind is that all of this may evolve and change over time, but this begins your roadmap towards achieving your "Why" and ultimately fulfilling your purpose. As you go through life, your viewpoints may shift and change, based on the fact that reality is always developing. Be sure to feel comfortable adjusting your who, what, when, why, and how as the market and purpose advance.

Evaluating Your Risk Factor Tolerance

My childhood friend, Jennifer, was someone that many would categorize as possessing an "entrepreneurial pedigree." She was the one who organized our bake sale fundraisers and ran for class president. She was someone we all looked up to as having the potential to become the first woman president. Jennifer went on to a top five business school and participated in internships with several top Fortune 500 companies.

After her college graduation, we all thought that she was one step away from launching the next Silicon Valley start-up or at the minimum would be leading one. We were shocked when we found out that she decided to enter a management training program with a popular car rental company. Please don't get me wrong—she took a major position in her organization, but we always thought she was the next Mark Zuckerberg or Meg Whitman.

I went out to lunch with her right after she took the job, and I asked her point-blank, "Jennifer, why did you settle for the management training position?"

Jennifer replied sternly, "Brandon, I didn't settle for anything."

She was plainly upset. Upon reflection, I later regretted what I said. I ultimately realized that I had been very invalidating of her new job venture. I think I just had a very specific vision in my mind for her future. But it was my vision—not hers.

What I failed to recognize was that Jennifer was a very calculated risk-taker. At this point in her career, she was simply not ready to take a big leap of faith. Instead she desired a calculated step. She wanted to join a company that would give her a structured learning experience where she knew what was around each and every corner in the process.

Sometimes we forget that we all address risk differently. Jennifer may well still turn out to become the first female president, or do anything she chooses. Really! The learning lesson for me, however, was that different people embrace risk in different ways at different times of their life. There is no right or wrong, but it is essential to evaluate your risk tolerance and comfort zone as it relates to your entrepreneurial spirit.

Picking Your Tendencies: Poker or Roulette

As you begin to evaluate your risk tolerance, I urge you to visualize it as if you are walking into a casino. When launching an entrepreneurial venture, there is always a risk. Hopefully, your private practice odds are calculated much higher in your favor than sitting down at a roulette table in Vegas.

One of the essential strategies for identifying your optimum business model is understanding your risk tolerance and the conditions under which you execute at your highest level. For example, my childhood friend, Jennifer, executes at her highest level under a very calculated and controlled risk environment. I have met others that thrive off the adrenaline of risk. Please keep in mind that some of the greatest entrepreneurs took huge risks and leaps of faith along with failures before they found success.

If you were walking into a casino and knew you were planning to gamble $1,000, which game would you play first? Are you the type that spends the $1,000 in the first night or the one that spreads out your $1,000 over the entire stay? Do you go into the game with the mindset that you might lose it all or with the expectation that you are going to walk away with a check that is equivalent to your annual salary?

It is essential to identify your tendencies when you address risk and understand how you execute at your highest capacity. One of the common mistakes that I find in entrepreneurs is they change their tendencies as they find success. As the saying goes, "Pigs get fat, and hogs get slaughtered." Just because you are $1,000 up on the house does not mean that you should increase your betting strategy. You need to know when to walk away from the bet.

One of the entrepreneurs that I worked with in the early stages of my career reached a lot of success early on. Unfortunately, her success brought a confidence where she changed up her tendencies and dumped a lot of money into a new venture because she thought the money would automatically buy additional success. Her failure to stay disciplined in her previous winning strategies cost her millions of dollars. When I confronted her on her recent failure, she shared with me that she let success change her winning recipe.

Each and every entrepreneurial venture requires its own analysis process and your tendencies when approaching risk should be monitored in the same light. You should calculate your risk, create your strategy, and execute it with an understanding of when it is time to walk away from the poker table.

Breaking Down the Self: Internal SWOT Analysis

As an entrepreneur begins to identify one's vision and uncover his or her natural tendencies, it is integral to break it all down and examine the intricate parts. Just as a mechanic breaks down an engine to examine barriers to efficiency, an entrepreneur must introspectively examine one's skill sets, weaknesses, and barriers to success.

One strategy to accomplish this is performing a SWOT analysis on yourself. A SWOT analysis is a common tool utilized to evaluate an opportunity, organization, or in this case the entrepreneur's "Strengths, Weaknesses, Opportunities, and Threats." Through this process, you will be able to strategize on ways to overcome any weakness areas or threats.

An example of a SWOT analysis framework:

Strength		Weakness
I **N** **T** **E** **R** **N** **A** **L**	Examples: Special expertise, special certifications, reputation, technology advantages, location advantages, languages, etc.	Examples: Limited clinical experience with certain demographics, marketing deficiencies, management of staff problems, lacking financial analytical skillset, etc.

Opportunities		Threats
E **X** **T** **E** **R** **N** **A** **L**	Examples: Underserved demographic in need of your services, lack of clinicians in the market that have your experience, funding opportunities, etc.	Examples: New or increased competition, insurance plan changes, adverse demographic changes, adverse govt. policies, economic slowdowns, etc.

Overall, the SWOT analysis will provide you and your business model with the necessary data to create an effective strategic plan. I run a SWOT analysis on myself, my business models, and new insurance contracts because it gives me the necessary foresight to prepare and strategize around internal and external circumstances so that I can be successful.

Identifying Your "Out-Strategy" and Your "Breaking Point"

In addition to the blank stares I get when I inquire about financial revenue goals from private practice entrepreneurs, I receive similar facial expressions when I ask about their proposed "out-strategy" and "breaking point."

I know that it can be a very confusing question since you have not even launched your private practice and I am already requesting your "exit strategy"! However, this is a necessity in understanding and identifying your business model. It may change over time, but the more defined your "out-strategy" and "breaking point" are, the more strategic you can be with goal setting, execution strategy, and aligning your business creativity within your risk tolerance comfort zone.

I typically recommend that you position your "out-strategy" into two primary questions.

The first question is: If you were to reach your optimum success in this business model, what would it look like and how would you want to exit the business? (Do you want to sell, do you want to set up a succession plan, etc.)

The next question is: If your business model was failing, how much money are you willing to risk before closing it down and what are the milestones along the way that will force you to change your approach?

The answers to both of these questions will provide you with essential metrics to track so that you can position the company to handle both success and adversity.

When I go to Vegas, I have a clear target of the financial success that I want to hit before I walk away from the game and the financial loss that will force me to stop playing the game.

Ultimately, entrepreneurship is a game of risk, purpose, and opportunity. The stakes are higher than in Vegas, but I still apply that same mindset of knowing when I have met my goals. As you identify the entrepreneur within you, you will be able to build a business model that is centered on purpose and a clear path for success.

CHAPTER 2

Navigating the Private Practice Environment

"It's kind of fun to do the impossible."
—Walt Disney

Through trials and tribulations, one may get feedback from those around them about their "luck." As we evaluate one's fortunate circumstances, adversity, and challenges, I believe that the following parable entitled: "Good Luck or Bad Luck" (from a Zen koan) gives an interesting perspective and goes as follows:

Once upon the time, there was an old farmer who had worked his crops for many years. One day his horse ran away. Upon hearing the news, his neighbors came to visit. "Such bad luck," they said sympathetically.

"Perhaps," the farmer replied.

The next morning the horse returned, bringing with it three other wild horses.

"What great luck!" the neighbors exclaimed.

"Perhaps," replied the old man.

The following day, his son tried to ride one of the untamed horses,

*was thrown, and broke his leg. The neighbors again came to offer their
sympathy on his misfortune.*

"Perhaps," answered the farmer.

*The day after, military officials came to the village to draft young
men into the army. Seeing that the son's leg was broken, they passed
him by. The neighbors congratulated the farmer on how well things
had turned out.*

"Perhaps," said the farmer...

Throughout your private practice journey, you are going to
have positive and negative circumstances impact the condition
and survival of your private practice. Please keep in mind that this
is normal.

From establishing a lucrative new funding source to payer
sources delaying their payment extensively, the key is not to judge
the circumstance by a philosophical label "good luck or bad luck,"
but to identify the strategies for creating more of the positive and
overcoming and preventing the negative. The private practice
environment is always evolving, and through my experience
consulting with practice owners all of the country, I have found
that those suffering from what they consider "bad luck" often stems
from a lack of preparation and understanding of the factors that are
influencing the private practice environment.

The Healthcare System and Its Impact on Your Private Practice

Understanding the healthcare system and its internal and
external impact as it relates to your community is integral to
navigating the private practice environment. As you go through
this book, you will begin to identify your pros and cons related to
working within the healthcare system as a private practice owner
and contracting with health insurance companies.

Regardless of your decision, you must realize that understanding
the healthcare system is essential no matter what. One of the core

benefits of understanding the healthcare system is that it will prepare you to create your value proposition to your potential clientele regardless if you are "in-network," "cash pay," or something else.

Private practice is made up of a multitude of moving parts—and the healthcare environment is constantly impacting how effective those moving parts may run. Have you ever noticed all of the maintenance that is recommended for your vehicle? When you purchase a car, you get a binder from the manufacturer of all their recommended maintenance as well as their warranties. It typically includes what services need to be performed every 3k miles, 10k miles, and so on. In addition, the binder shares the meaning behind the different alerts they have on your dashboard such as lights that come on to trigger when there is an electronic or mechanical problem or when maintenance is needed.

In today's cars, you even get a light that turns on when your tires are low on pressure. When you think about it, the resources that are given to you in the hopes of getting the most out of your vehicle are pretty amazing.

As I think about all of the details of the maintenance requirements for a successful private practice, I realize that there is an essential need for private practice owners to have a dashboard of their own with alerts, maintenance checklists, and more. This maintenance binder includes everything from business growth strategy development to performing annual compliance audits. One of the key maintenance items that I always recommend is understanding and navigating the current legislation and proposed changes related to the current healthcare initiatives.

We live in a time of considerable turmoil, doubt, and insecurity; therefore, it is essential for private practice owners to be aware of the past and present and advocate for the future regardless of your payer mix.

The Evolution of Healthcare Reform

First and foremost, it is essential to realize that health insurance reform and the role of government on the impact of the healthcare system in the United States has been a major political debate since the early part of the 20th century.

One of the challenges is that there are two major conflicting ideologies on the spectrum, and the United States of America has long been torn over identifying the proper solution.

On the left side of ideologies, we have a group advocating for a "Socialized Healthcare System" in which everyone receives healthcare and taxes cover all expenses; such a structure resembles healthcare systems in Europe, Israel, and most industrialized countries.

The other ideology on the right side is that healthcare is not the responsibility of the government and that ultimately it should be a free market.

On March 23, 2010, President Obama signed the Federal Patient Protection and Affordable Care Act also referred to as the Affordable Care Act (ACA). Without adopting a partisan viewpoint, there have been pros and cons in the role of the ACA's impact on our healthcare industry and society. One of the biggest benefits from the ACA as it relates to society is that "pre-existing conditions" may not limit someone from qualifying for healthcare insurance coverage based on the ACA guidelines, but please keep in mind that major provisions of the ACA are currently in the process of being challenged by the Trump administration.

Provisions included in the ACA were intended to expand access to insurance, increase consumer protections, emphasize prevention and wellness, improve quality and system performance, expand the health workforce, and control the rising health care expenses.

It is obvious that one of the largest impacts that the 2010 Affordable Care Act had in our country is the requirement for millions of uninsured citizens to get health care coverage. According to the Henry Kaiser Family Foundation, there were 47 million Americans—nearly 18 percent of the population—without health insurance coverage prior to 2010.

There are benefits and challenges to the change in having millions of Americans obtain healthcare insurance; one of the challenges stems from the infrastructure of our healthcare system.

As health insurance became mandatory, the insurance companies gained an advantage as well as challenges. The advantage was that the demand for insurance coverage shifted in their favor; the challenge was that more and more Americans were utilizing their healthcare insurance. In most cases, insurance companies are hoping to gain financial premiums without the expenses.

When you purchase "flood insurance," the premiums are initially quoted with the expectation that it is highly unlikely that the policy would be utilized. There is obviously a risk, but insurance companies anticipate that the majority of their subscribers will not need the insurance coverage. Due to the increase in healthcare utilization, insurance companies began increasing annual healthcare premiums while reducing provider reimbursement.

This ultimately resulted in America being challenged with a healthcare identity crisis. The Affordable Care Act was ultimately not affordable because expenses were continuing to grow while the quality of care went down in many cases due to a reduction in funding.

As I meet people throughout the United States, I have grown increasingly passionate about surveying their viewpoint on our current healthcare system. What I have learned is that there is no perfect system and that we don't have a "maintenance guide" for making our healthcare system work. My personal belief is that the investment in preventative health will ultimately be the key to the "maintenance guide" for running an effective healthcare system.

In addition, the key to making it better is through accountability for healthcare outcomes. At the end of the day, our healthcare system is a business, and it will continue to be run like a business regardless of the role that government plays in it. My personal belief is that the key to success in today's healthcare environment is clear communication, transparency, and the ability to ensure the best return on investment for consumers. As the old saying goes, "You get what you pay for."

Understanding Insurance Plans

As a private practice entrepreneur—AKA "private practice-preneur"—begins to explore the role they want to play in the healthcare environment, they must really understand the funding model of health insurance and how healthcare insurance works. The first fundamental that all private practice-preneurs must realize is that there is never a "guarantee of coverage."

If you have never verified insurance coverage before, I want you to do a little exercise where you call the phone number on the back of your health insurance card and verify your own benefits for whatever service you are interested in offering (Occupational Therapy, Physical Therapy, Speech Therapy, Chiropractic, Nutrition, Behavioral Therapy, and so on).

In addition to finding out the benefit, I want you to ask if there are any exceptions or restrictions related to the benefit. By the end of your phone call, I am confident that you will realize that your phone call was essentially someone reading a page from your benefits policy. It is a common story at many offices across the country.

At the end of the day, there is no guarantee of coverage, and there is limited responsibility the insurance company takes in covering payment for the services.

I share this perspective with you not to scare you out of working with health insurance, but to prepare you to implement systems and strategies for success.

Our society has a widespread misunderstanding that just because your health insurance says the service is a "covered benefit," your insurance company guarantees they will pay the bill. Unfortunately, there are many loopholes in the funding of healthcare services, and it is far from a black and white system.

Due to the lack of financial guarantees, the most valuable thing that a private practice-preneur can do is under-promise and over-deliver with their clientele. You never want your customer to feel that the health insurance company is guaranteed to cover the services. You want to explain your processes, the patient's liability and risk, and ultimately the timeline for identifying when a claim has been successfully paid.

As I troubleshoot funding issues for private practices on a regular basis, I have found that most are not aware that your contract does not guarantee that every service gets funded. I have surveyed the top billing companies and billing departments throughout the country and found that the best collection rate that I found is 97 percent. That means in the best-case scenario, you should anticipate you may not get paid on three percent of the claims you submit. I have met a handful of practices that state they get paid 100 percent of the time. However, their claims are less than 500 per year, which is extremely small. Please keep in mind that the more variables you have in your private practice, the harder it is to reach 100 percent success in claims being paid.

As just one example, the Orthopedic Physical Therapy practice that submits 50 insurance claims per month is more likely to get 100 percent of those claims paid than the Pediatric Practice that is submitting 250 claims per month inclusive of Occupational Therapy, Physical Therapy, and Speech Therapy with a varied range of diagnosis. The reason it can be challenging at times to prove medical necessity for pediatric services is that some deem the services as "educational" and not "medical" depending on the diagnosis, documentation, doctor's notes, and other factors.

The bottom line is that you must understand the limiting factors and trends related to medical billing depending on your patient demographics, diagnosis, service offering, etc.

Some core keywords to remember related to insurance:

Deductible – The dollar amount per year (either calendar year or plan year) that a given health insurance subscriber (patient) has to pay for his or her medical expenses before insurance begins to reimburse for expenses. Please keep in mind that not all services are "subject to a deductible" and not all plans have a deductible. If the patient has a deductible, it will reset every year. Depending on the plan, it may reset on the calendar year (January 1st), or it may reset on the plan year renewal, which is when your plan renews based on the initiation of the policy.

Copayment – This is a fixed flat fee that patient's insurance plan may have in the policy as a "per visit fee." Please keep in mind that copayments can range from $5 per visit to $70 per visit depending on the plan. Typically a patient will either have a "copayment" or a "coinsurance."

Co-insurance – Some plans utilize a coinsurance for patient's responsibility instead of a copayment. Therefore, it is a percentage of the bill that the patient pays versus a flat visit amount. Example: Insurance may cover 70 percent of the visit rate. Therefore, the patient is responsible for 30 percent of the visit's cost.

Out-Of-Pocket Maximum – This is the most that a plan subscriber should pay for benefit covered services during a policy period before the insurance company covers 100 percent of covered services. The co-insurance will change once the out-of-pocket maximum has been satisfied.

Surcharge – If you are an in-network provider, then your contract with the insurance company will identify that you are not allowed to charge extra patient fees on top of the contracted rate to perform the contracted service. That extra charge would be identified as a surcharge. If you are out-of-network, then you are not bound by the same surcharge regulations.

Explanation of Benefits (EOB) – A statement sent by a health insurance company to covered individuals explaining what medical treatments and/or services were paid for on their behalf. The "EOB" is commonly attached to a check or statement of electronic payment.

Verification of Benefits (VOB) – An evaluation of coverage as it relates to a patient's services. Within a verification of benefits, a patient can find out if the service is a covered benefit. They can also identify their plan deductible, co-insurance, copayment, out of pocket max, etc.

Contracted Charges – These are the reimbursement rates that are negotiated in a provider's contract and what they are anticipating to receive in total reimbursement for the service. The contracted rate is the gross rate of what the provider should receive from the insurance company and client together.

Billed Charges – These are the charges that a provider bills insurances when they submit claims. The billed charges are typically higher than the contracted rates. Therefore, they do not reflect what you should be making per visit. These are generally higher because some insurance contracts don't identify a flat reimbursement rate but rather a percentage of billed charges.

Aging Report – An accounts receivable aging is a report that lists unpaid claims based on date ranges. This is the most common report that a billing department runs to see any claims submitted when payment is not received along with the length of time that they are outstanding.

"To Be In-Network or Not To Be In-Network"... That Is the Question

This is truly the million-dollar question that I hear from practically every private practice that I consult for and meet with. You may not like my answer, but it is the only one that I feel confident giving you—and that answer is "it depends."

As you begin to develop your private practice vision, the strategic goals and risk tolerance, you will begin to identify the capacity of which you should work with health insurances.

There is one key metric that I always recommend for all scalable private practices regardless of the path you choose related to working with private healthcare insurances as a payer source. That rule of thumb is that 60 percent of your funding should be cash flow positive in 30 days or less from the date of service.

Let me elaborate to ensure that this metric makes sense. If you perform 1,000 billable units between all of your funding sources for the month of January, then you should receive payment in full for 60 percent by the end of February, in order to run a cash flow positive business. I also recommend that the 40 percent of the revenue that you are not collecting within thirty days from the date of service have a profit margin of at least 30 percent above your gross expense. The bottom line is that these metrics will keep your private practice financially moving in the right direction and help you run a sustainable business.

In addition to performing a "SWOT" analysis on the role that health insurance should play in your private practice, I think it is essential for you to understand your options related to accepting insurance or not.

Here is a sample breakdown of different options:

Become an In-Network Private Insurance Provider. This means that you are contracted with a commercial health insurance company or network in which you agree to their guidelines, restrictions, and contracted rates. Things to look out for:

- There are no guarantees of payment, so be sure to understand your contract structure and terms related to holding a patient responsible for a claim that is denied.

- Ensure that you create relationships with a network manager, case management director, and person is leadership related to your contract to troubleshoot any issues.

- Keep in mind that your contract prohibits any form of up-charge that they classify as a "surcharge." Therefore, you must negotiate in your contract your rights, such as charging a "cancellation penalty."

Become a Medicare or Medicaid Provider. Please keep in mind that becoming a Medicare Provider and a Medicaid Provider are separate processes. Please note that becoming a Medicare-approved Provider or a Medicaid-approved Provider may be a necessity for being able to contract with certain commercial health insurance companies. There are some things to stay on the lookout for:

- Keep in mind that some commercial contracts will hold you to the Medicaid rate when you are a "Medicaid Approved Provider."

- Understand the claim submission time requirements to get paid by either Medicaid or Medicare. Also, ensure that you are in compliance with all of the guidelines set forth by CMS—the Centers for Medicare & Medicaid Services. You can learn more by visiting www.cms.gov.

Provide In-Network Benefits While Not Being A Traditional In-Network Contracted Provide. There are times when an insurance network does not have the appropriate provider network in a given region. Therefore, they will allow clients to see an out-of-network provider and offer either a "letter of agreement" or allow in-network benefits to the patient via a "gap exception."

In simplest terms, a network gap exception is a tool health insurance companies use to compensate for gaps in their network. This allows an out-of-network provider to get their fee schedule and not be held to the "in-network" contract while providing patients a lower fee by giving in-network benefits.

Provide Cash-Pay Services as Out-Of-Network Provider but Offer a "Superbill." Some private practices offer their clients a service called a "superbill," which is a charge slip with itemized charges and codes patients can submit to their insurance company for potential reimbursement via out-of-network benefits. Things to look out for:

- Patients sometimes assume that insurance is guaranteed to reimburse when a superbill is submitted. Make certain you have a policy explaining that the private practice holds no responsibility or liability related to a patient being reimbursed by a private practice.

- There are private practices that try to bill claims as an out-of-network provider on behalf of their patient in which they have challenges getting paid because payments will often go directly to the patient. My recommendation is never expect an insurance company to pay a private practice directly unless you are an in-network provider.

- The reason that many private practices opt to become an in-network provider is that they unlock a much larger network of patients. As you begin to identify your private practice goals, scalability, and cash flow requirements, you will be able to determine the role that you want to play in accepting private insurance as a funding source. Ultimately, understanding the healthcare system and its impact on your private practice is a necessity when navigating the current private practice environment so that you can reach optimum success.

Secrets to Changing a Reality

Our perceptions of reality impact our success, day in and day out. I find that a lack of reality or false perception of reality is the #1 reason for private practices failing in today's environment. Reality is defined as "the world or the state of things as they actually exist, as opposed to an idealistic or notional idea of them." If we walk outside and I say the sky is blue and you say the sky is gray, our perception of the reality is plainly different. A difference, in the perception of reality, does not just impact the survival of your private practice, but may also be the number one cause of conflict in communication, which impacts patient care and your private practice business model.

Defining Your Current Private Practice Reality

I recently was consulting with a woman named Sophia who was a Speech Language Pathologist. She was planning on relocating from Seattle to California and opening up a new private practice.

As we began our first consultation together, I realized that Sophia was making decisions based on a false perception of reality.

First and foremost, Sophia made the cardinal mistake of not navigating the private practice environment in her newly proposed region of California. Therefore, her perception of reality was based 100 percent on her experience in Seattle. In addition to not being prepared for several compliance guidelines, Sophia assumed that her insurance reimbursement for her services would be the same in California as it was in her old market.

She became shocked and panicked when I explained to her that the reimbursement for Blue Cross of California patients was 40 percent less than she was used to receiving. She rapidly became defensive and angry. As we went through the discovery process, I was able to bring facts to the table that empowered her to understand and embrace the reality of California's private practice environment.

By recognizing and embracing a new perception of reality, she was able to prepare and strategize for a much more successful approach to opening up a private practice in California. It is essential for private practice owners to identify their current perception of a private practice reality and utilize facts to recognize any faults in your reality. It is necessary that you don't just follow hearsay but identify the truth through factual data. Just as clinicians do research on "outcome measured clinical approaches," private practice owners must do research to find the facts related to navigating the private practice environment.

Common Misnomers in Today's Private Practice Environment

First and foremost, I want to ensure that you understand that a "misnomer" is a wrong or inaccurate name, designation, or understanding. One of the reasons that I love consulting and speaking in front of clinicians throughout the United States is because I get to learn so much about the differences in private practice environment from each regional area.

I find that there are often misnomers or misunderstandings that impact a private practice owner's perception of reality on a regular basis. I often find that private practice owners assume that the private practices are faced with the same circumstances in every region, but that is actually a misnomer. I have now consulted with hundreds of private practice owners in the United States, and I must share that there are no two identical scenarios. Although there are similar challenges and frustrations, each and every private practice owner is embracing different circumstances and realities.

Another common misnomer is that a "cash-pay" private practice is easier to operate than an "insurance-funded" private practice. There are definitely factors that are easier in a "cash-pay" private practice, but there are also factors in an "insurance-funded" practice that are easier.

The reality is that each type of private practice has circumstances that are easier and more challenging, but you can't make a general assumption that one way is easier than the other. It all comes down to creating systems for the type of private practice you are running and utilizing appropriate metrics to hold the business model accountable to your success strategy.

My favorite misnomer that I am faced with frequently is I find that clinicians open up private practices and assume immediate success because the demand for their services is so high. I know several clinicians that opened up private practices and justified it to me saying, "Brandon, I have 100 patients on my waiting list, so why is my private practice failing?"

Private practices fail based on a broken business model and false financial expectations, which result in cash flow challenges, profitability challenges, and so on. It is essential to recognize that running a successful private practice is implementing an efficient and effective business model regardless of the supply and demand benefits.

Slow and Steady Wins the Race

As you navigate the private practice environment, you will begin to recognize barriers to success. There is such a thing as "scaling too fast." It sounds silly that an organization may fail because they grow too fast, but it is actually a common occurrence. For example, if a private practice has two full-time clinicians, and they triple their clinical team within a week, they may hit a major cash-flow challenge if their payroll increases so fast where their accounts receivable may be delayed due to the funding source.

My favorite saying is that private practice success is truly a "marathon" in which you must pace yourself. There are very few private practices that survive if they grow faster than their means can provide. Therefore, I recommend that you have a calculated growth strategy where slow and steady wins you the race.

Overcoming Obstacles as a Private Practice-Preneur

In the words of the famous, French playwright Moliere, "The greater the obstacle, the more glory in overcoming it."

This world is made up of obstacles, barriers, and adversity. As a private practice-preneur, you will find that it is a necessity to develop the analytical ability to overcome these obstacles. As a private practice-preneur, you are developing new tools every day to succeed. The key to overcoming an obstacle is to step back and gain perspective on the cause of the obstacle.

The Most Common Private Practice Obstacles

One of the common obstacles that I find with private practice-preneurs is they recruit their friends to work for them. I believe this can be extremely dangerous even when everyone has the best of intentions. Please keep in mind that I am not one to speak as I work with both family and friends, but there are obstacles that arise due to the relationship.

I have had multiple private practice owners that have suffered with a similar story.

Mary is a Physical Therapist who opened her private practice in 2008. Mary was excited because one of her close buddies, Lisa, joined her practice in 2010 and became the lead Occupational Therapist. Over the years, Mary has given compensation increases to Lisa.

However, in 2015, Lisa reached her financial ceiling, and Mary cannot afford to give her any more increases because she would lose money on Lisa's therapy. Mary explained to Lisa that she could not afford to give more increases, but Lisa just could not understand why other private practices were able to pay more. Mary tried to explain the circumstances, but Lisa felt like Mary should reduce the private practice's net income to retain her. Lisa also felt that Mary should not be able to make money from her services. Ever since Mary declined Lisa's compensation increase request, things have felt a little bit awkward, and the friendship is not what it was in previous years.

In 2017, Lisa gave Mary two weeks notice and left for a higher pay clinic position. This situation brings up several obstacles that private practice-preneurs are faced with:

- Hiring a friend and the business side impacting the relationship

- Employees not recognizing that a private practice should make a profit from their services

- Employees leaving a caseload with only two weeks notice

These three obstacles have impacted many of the clients that I work with. I believe the solution to overcome these obstacles is communication. Through your communication, you must separate the relationship into three categories:

- Business (Be transparent about financial expectations, private practice financial goals, etc.)

- Clinical (Discuss the clinical expectations for the relationship. Explain how to overcome clinical caseload abandonment and responsibility as a clinician.)

- Personal (Discuss that the key to a strong personal relationship is being transparent with expectations to the above two categories.)

If I could change one thing about our society's viewpoint on service-based business models related to healthcare, it would be their viewpoint on private healthcare practices running their model as a successful and profitable business model. I still don't understand why society thinks it is a conflict of interest for someone who is saving lives to be a millionaire. Going back to my intro chapter, why can't a private practice-preneur make the same kind of money as "The Rock"?

The Secrets to Executing Your Private Practice Strategy

As you navigate the private practice environment and begin to create a strategic plan, you must also recognize that the secret to executing a plan is in accountability. Have you ever been to a conference and leave feeling empowered, excited, and motivated only to be stuck in the same position a month later? The problem is that it is easy to get motivated and easy to create a plan, but it is challenging to execute the plan and achieve goals. Studies show that the vast majority of Americans making New Year's resolutions focus on setting fitness goals—only for the vast majority to give up on them.

The bottom line is that naming your private practice strategy is only part of the equation, but executing it is the secret to success. The secret to executing your private practice strategy is in creating accountability through metrics. I recommend that you develop weekly, monthly, and quarterly metrics as it relates to the execution of your private practice strategy. In addition, you must always be open to reevaluating your strategy to ensure that it is appropriate given the current private practice environment.

Why Most Private Practices Fail

As I navigate the private practice environment throughout the United States through consultations and speaking engagements, I recognize that there is a very high failure rate.

I have found that the only industry with a higher failure rate that I have personally noticed is within the restaurant industry. The number one reason for private practices failing in today's environment is they are simply not identifying their risk factors. Nor are they building a support team to help with essential decision-making. I believe that the most successful private practices have a core team, and that team may be made up of employees, owners, volunteers, consultants, and family.

In addition, I have found that most private practices that failed have underestimated the resources that are needed for a successful practice. They have not conducted their due-diligence. As you build your strategy, you need a team that will watch over your shoulder. You must be prepared for even the worst conditions impacting your survival.

Ask yourself:

- What do you do if you have a low client satisfaction rate?

- Do you have a lawyer reviewing all of your employment and legal documents?

- What is the cost of a failed compliance audit such as a HIPAA breach?

- Is your practice labor intensive?

- How do you handle your best therapist going into competition with you by opening up his or her own private practice?

- What if your funding source stops making payments? What is your strategy to fix the solution if they make up 80 percent of your revenue? (e.g. Medicaid, etc.)

- What are your anticipated fixed expenses?

- What are your anticipated variable expenses?

- What KPIs are integral to the survival of your private practice?

Phew! Yes, you must be prepared to answer all of these questions.

Too often than not, private practice-preneurs look like a "deer in headlights" when I ask these questions. The reason why private practices fail is they are not prepared.

As a private practice-preneur prepares to launch a new private practice or scale their private practice, there is no benefit in identifying the results as "good luck or bad luck" but rather what contributed to the results. A private practice-preneur must recognize the importance of navigating the private practice environment through examining the healthcare environment, their perspectives on reality, and their strategies for recognizing and overcoming obstacles. The end result is a calculated process that includes accountability and a defined result that you label as success.

CHAPTER 3

The Ethics Dilemma: Black and White or Lots of Gray?

"Honesty is the cornerstone of all success.
Without honesty, confidence and ability to perform
shall cease to exist."
—Mary Kay Ash

As you progress through your private practice journey, you will face adversity on numerous occasions, and I have found that adversity is one of the contributing factors that helps us define our moral compass or ethics.

Through my career, I have been faced on several occasions with the realization that my business lenses or moral compass is often closer to "black and white" viewpoints as it relates to compliance and "grays" when it comes to solving problems. You will find that there are private practices that operate in ways that don't align with your ethics or moral compass, and it is important to define your lenses from the beginning. Your lenses may be defined based on the category, but it is essential to also understand the moral compass for your team members.

In many cases, people's ethics or moral capacity are defined based on the repercussions for their actions. As I approach adversity, I always look at the different ways to handle a situation and it reminds me of a classic Aesop's Fable called "*The Sun and the North Wind.*"

Once upon a time, the North Wind and the Sun had an argument. Each thought he was stronger than the other. "There's only one thing for it, "said the North Wind. "We'll have to put our strength together. We'll have a competition."

He pointed to a traveler, walking along a road far below them, on the face of the world. "See that man?"

The Sun nodded.

"See the coat he's wearing?"

"Yes, I can see his coat."

"Well, whichever one of us can strip the coat from his back will have proved himself the strongest."

The Sun smiled and nodded. "Very well, Wind. You go first."

So the North Wind began to blow. He came whirling down out of the sky and set the man's coat flapping, so the traveler buttoned it up. He blew harder, as though he could tear it from the man's back, but the traveler thrust his hands into his pockets and held the coat closer. He blew with all of his strength, but the traveler bent himself against the wind and held his coat tighter still. For all his puffing and panting, the wind could do nothing.

Then it was the Sun's turn. The wind stopped, the clouds parted and the Sun shone. He shone gently at first, so the traveler relaxed his stride and unfastened his buttons. Then he shone more fiercely; the traveler took off his coat and slung it over his shoulder. Then the Sun shone with all of his strength; the traveler threw his coat onto the ground and sat under the shade of a tree.

The Sun turned to the North Wind. "So, who's stronger? You or me?"

Just as in this parable, we often find our greatest results through persuasion rather than sheer force of strength. It can be much more effective and far more sustainable to inspire our people to take action through offering them incentives and encouragement, rather than strong-arming them.

Unfortunately, it doesn't always quite work that way when it comes to regulatory measures from the government. I know that in our heart of hearts, most of us strive to do the right thing. Most of us set out to live ethical lives, particularly those of us in service-oriented fields (i.e. healthcare providers, teachers, therapists, etc.) who have often made very serious oaths to that effect. And yet those intentions are not enough; we also need to ensure that we are in the utmost ethical compliance with government requirements, particularly when it comes to how we treat our employees. Let's walk through a few examples.

Identifying the Compliance Factors that Matter

In addition to the range of other health and business factors you need to keep in mind, you also need to get up to speed on identifying key compliance factors that could otherwise spell out major trouble for your business if not followed closely.

There are a variety of small business and private practice compliance factors that each owner should be aware of. Let's review a few of them.

Human Resources Compliance

These include such matters as:

- Labor laws

- Legal regulations

- Operations

- HIPAA

Some might question whether HIPAA should truly be considered under the umbrella of human resources. Part of the reasoning here is that when confidential medical information is leaked, it is a workforce issue—naturally falling under the jurisdiction of HR resource compliance.

Government Funding Compliance

Every program you will interact with, from Medicare and Medicaid to state programs, will have their own compliance factors that you will need to have a firm grasp on. You will be responsible for ensuring any auditing requirements, for example, are necessary. One of my programs is state-funded and requires several audits annually. We conduct a financial audit based on our state funding requirement in order to demonstrate that 85 percent of our revenue is used directly for the care of clientele, as required. Other regular audits focus on quality of outcomes and documentation.

HR Best Practices

I firmly believe that this is one area that many new private practice owners neglect—and at their great peril.

Regulations

There are four legal levels of labor law regulations that will likely impact you:

- Federal

- State

- County

- City

Depending on where you live, the strictness of the regulations will vary. At the end of the day, you are responsible for following the strictest regulations that you fall under.

For example, California probably has the highest amount of compliance regulations for HR of any state. Furthermore, there are cities and counties across that have even higher regulations than the state standard.

I always tell people that it's very rare in the state of California that a federal regulation will be equivalent to a state or city regulation; it will almost always be higher in the state of California and cities within California than any federal regulation. For example, the city of Santa Monica has one of the strictest HR regulations that you have to keep in mind.

The same is true in San Francisco and San Jose, which have stricter minimum wage, stricter labor law requirements, and stricter compliance factors—all factors to keep in mind.

If a business delivers services in Los Angeles, you must follow the Los Angeles regulations regarding "paid sick leave" regardless of where the office headquarters is or the employee resides because it benefits the employees that are delivering services in that jurisdiction. Based in Los Angeles, my company delivers therapy services throughout Southern California. We found that even though we have people covering much of California, the majority of our workforce was delivering services throughout the city of Los Angeles. For us, rather than having different compliance factors, we just followed the strictest regulations across the board throughout our California locations; that's a decision that you may look at as well.

Current Labor Law Regulations Impacting Private Practices Throughout the United States

One of the labor law regulations that most small businesses don't realize is the difference between exempt employees and non-exempt employees. As a result of classification and misclassification, lawsuits are on the rise.

Exempt employees are defined as "employees who, based on duties performed and manner of compensation, shall be exempt from the Fair Labor Standards Act (FLSA) minimum wage and overtime provisions." These are employees that are paid a "salary." There are common misnomers about exempt salaried roles and employers don't realize that there are strict guidelines to qualify for the classification of "exempt employee" and receive a guaranteed salary.

(To dive deeper into this topic, you can visit https://www. hr.ucsb.edu/what-exempt-employee-or-position.)

Three of the most common classifications for exempt salaried are administrative exemption, executive exemption, and professional exemption. Overall, you must pass the exemption qualified requirements to fall under the exempt classification. The reason is that the IRS and DOL are concerned that employers may classify someone as exempt if ultimately the employee is working more than 40 hours of work without proper compensation, rest breaks, meal breaks, etc. An example of an appropriate exempt classification would be a physician under the professional exemption. The physician may have a set salary of $200,000 annually. She may work 30 hours per week certain weeks and 60 hours per week on other weeks; however, her compensation is a guaranteed salary of $200,000 per year regardless of hours worked.

Exempt employees are defined as an employee who is entitled to overtime pay and minimum wage as described in the Fair Labor Standards Act (FLSA). Non-exempt employees must be paid for

THE PRIVATE PRACTICE SURVIVAL GUIDE

each hour that they work and 1.5x their hourly wage for overtime, etc. Please keep in mind that if someone is an hourly employee, it does not mean that high compensation positions are not categorized under non-exempt roles. There are many high compensation positions that fall under this classification.

Many business owners out there are misclassifying employees as exempt because they want to forego overtime expenses and get the most from an employee. An example is a private practice hiring a front desk receptionist at an annual salary of $30,000 in which the employee is working an average of 50 hours per week, but he or she is not subject to any overtime. This employee will most likely be misclassified if you put them through the classification test and should be a non-exempt employee. If there was an audit, this could be extremely costly to the employer.

To combat this, the IRS and the Department of Labor have come together to set compliance measures and regulations clarifying issues involving exempt versus non-exempt employees.

It is important to understand overtime regulations in your state, city, and county because they can often be different. It is your responsibility to follow the strictest guidelines as applicable to your practice. In California, as an example, someone might qualify for time and a half following an eight-hour shift; whereas in Texas, their working time is measured in terms of the week, not the day.

Again, it is crucial to understand the guidelines in your jurisdiction. In terms of non-exempt employees who are paid hourly, they receive a number of protections, such as rest break and lunch requirements. My general rule of thumb is to provide these workers with a 15-minute break within the first three hours of their shift, an unpaid lunch for a minimum of 30 minutes where they are not doing any work, and an additional 15-minute break in the afternoon. As requirements shift and vary based on location, you will want to identify the optimal schedule for your workers and stick to it. Please be advised that the safest classification is as a "non-exempt" employee. The IRS and Department of Labor are looking for cases where employees are not getting proper compensation, proper reimbursement for rest and meal breaks, etc.

One of the areas in private practice that I find often have misclassifications is with the utilization of clinical assistants. I frequently find assistants in particular to be misclassified as exempt under the professional designation, which most labor attorneys would advise is incorrect classification. I find this all the time, especially with nursing assistants, certified occupational therapy assistants, and physical therapy therapist assistants. Be sure to brush up on the laws and regulations outlining these qualifications.

Some employees will receive what is called an executive or management designation. I personally qualify for such a designation, as I spend well over 50 percent of my time managing others. It is important that you run the classification tests on all employees so that you are protecting yourself from future lawsuits.

As these designations can quickly grow confusing, it may be best to err on the side of caution and generally pay everyone hourly and pay overtime under the non-exempt classification. Be sure to properly classify your talent and maintain careful records, as any misclassifications identified during an audit can open your business up to the risk of significant fines and back-owed wages.

Basic Employment Regulations to Keep in Mind

If you have between 1-14 employees, as seems to be common within the healthcare profession, there are some specific areas of employment regulation that you should especially keep in mind.

If you are offering health insurance, are you also offering COBRA, an acronym for the Consolidated Omnibus Budget Reconciliation Act? This law provides for the continuation of healthcare insurance in the event that an employee leaves your organization.

You should also pay special attention to:

- Child Labor Regulations

- Disability Insurance

- Discrimination

- Foreign Workers

- Discrimination Laws

- Employee Safety

- Fair Employment and Housing Act

- Immigration Reform and Control Act

- Military Leave

- New Employee Reporting

- Paid Family Leave

I would also urge you to take special care when it comes to the posters and notices distributed throughout your facilities. In 75 percent of the private practices that I audit, I often typically begin by closely looking at their labor posters—these highlight the minimum wage, guidelines for the state, and other similar information. Posting these has nothing to do with interior decoration—they are requirements mandated by the Department of Labor. You ignore posting these at your extreme peril. Be sure to place them where they will be highly visible to your employees, such as in the lunchroom or by a time clock to ensure that your entire team can see them.

You might ask if this is really all that necessary, depending on the size of your organization. "Brandon, I only have three employees! I can just tell them this information! It's silly to post it."

Believe me, I know. But you don't want to mess around with it. You are far better served to follow the rules if you want to stay safe in today's regulatory environment. Put the posters up and keep them up and updated. Posts are typically updated annually.

Pregnancy Disability Laws

Make special attention to making sure you follow the letter of these laws to the T. Playing it fast and loose with pregnancy and maternity leave-related matters is one of the quickest ways that you can ensure you will be sued. As a reminder, this falls under the protected class regulations and Family and Medical Leave Act of 1993.

Sexual Harassment Training

Are you offering it? You should be, especially in today's environment—you simply can't get away with not doing it. Every year you should be offering sexual harassment training.

Other issues you need to keep in mind include:

- Smoking in the Workplace

- Time Off

- Unemployment Insurance

- Wage and Hour Laws

- Workers' Compensation

- Employee Handbook

After I have private practices show me their posters, I most often then ask to see their employee handbook. All too often, I hear that they haven't taken the time to write one, or they basically printed a generic handbook off the internet.

This is a major mistake. Whenever I have consulted on a private practice that is embattled with labor law disputes, the employee handbook has been one of the missing ingredients to preventing the matter. I now take pride in staying on top of this as an important resource and tool. I actually learned this the hard way—or an embarrassing way.

When I joined one of my companies several years ago, I never realized the importance of an employee handbook as a compliance tool. I was given the employee handbook but did not carefully read it. This was obviously early on in my career prior to advancing my HR knowledge. I assumed the employee handbook was accurate and by the book—why wouldn't it be? As I grew into a leadership role within the organization, I did not put much attention on it until one day when I presented it to a recently hired HR Director named Tom. He asked me if we had a current employee handbook. I was excited to present it and with pride visible in my voice, I told him, "Boom, here you go." It was a suitably thick and dense handbook, chock full of detail.

Tom read it and asked to see me a week later. He asked me, "When was the last time you read the employee handbook?"

I laughed and looked at him awkwardly. With some embarrassment, I admitted that I had only skimmed it and our previous manager largely put it together based on some recommendations and online research.

Tom then asked me, "Brandon, can you point me to where your pay phone is located?"

I shot him a grin that expressed confusion on my face and replied, "We don't have a pay phone, Tom." He took a pause, and now I was getting nervous because he kept thoroughly looking down at our employee handbook.

He then picked his head up slowly and looked at me and said, "Well, in this handbook that you gave me, you say that your organization has a pay phone and all personal calls should be made from there. So you are in essence providing a handbook that doesn't reflect your company's policies." Obviously, this may seem like overkill to you, but Tom's point is that your employee handbook is your policies and procedures manual—and you must take every statement in your handbook very serious. Without a clear and accurate employee handbook, you don't have a leg to stand on in terms of a labor dispute, employee correction cycles, and other issues.

I have since learned just how important it is to ensure that guidelines to employees are as up to date and accurate as possible and that you must do your own due diligence before just implementing a cookie cutter compliance manual. I also now make sure that someone else reviews all of these communications to ensure they are correct—it can be very helpful to have an extra set of eyes to catch any glaring errors like this. This real-life story of Tom and I makes me laugh to this day, especially when I think that many kids today would not even know what a payphone is.

Some Essential HR Questions

- What are your financial thresholds?

- Are you giving employees sick time? Are you legally required?

- What's the minimum wage for your employees?

- Are you deducting the correct taxes from your employees' payroll checks?

- Do you have all 10 employees and legally required items on your payroll checks? Are you paying your employees in a timely manner?

Most states require that you pay an employee at least twice a month. Therefore, if you have W2 employees, you want to ensure that you are paying them, in most states, twice a month. I have found that often people will make that mistake and only pay once a month, but as a W2 employee, most states will require you to pay two times a month.

Do your employees perform work without getting paid? Is that legal? In our industry you have to understand the labor laws. It can be very easy to get caught up in the ethos of the gig economy in which we pay people often in global reimbursement vs. hourly reimbursement. If you hand out $100 to someone for a patient visit, for example, it might be looked at as paying them $100 an hour. But what if they are taking ten hours to carry out the task in terms of clinical documentation, client scheduling, clinical collaboration, and follow through? You can see how these matters can very quickly grow in complexity. I recommend meeting with an HR consultant or private practice consultant to troubleshoot these complexities with the goal of mitigating risk.

- If you offer health benefits, are you supplying them the required information about the health plans?

- Do you have a social media policy?

- Are you correctly completing your I-9s?

- Do you have I-9s for all your employees?

- How do bonuses affect the overtime?

I recently found that I was making an error with staff in California—I was paying overtime, without accounting for bonuses paid within the year. My HR team informed me that I needed to return to the books at the end of the year and conduct an audit to ensure that the overtime rate was appropriate—i.e., ensure that the hourly rate of staff was adjusted based on all of the bonuses paid out throughout the year. These are just some of the little things that we want to find out and intricacies to keep us safe.

Is sexual harassment training required? Usually it is, and if not, I strongly recommend it. This does not just concern sexual harassment between staff members, but also sexual harassment from patients. Sadly, I am sure that many of you have heard these stories. I have unfortunately seen it take place firsthand throughout my career, underscoring the need to have very robust policies in place.

- What's your meal and rest break policy?

- What laws do you have to comply with?

- Can your application form get you sued? Do you know that there are certain things that you can't ask any longer on an application?

- Do you know what you can and can't say during an interview?

- Are you giving the new proper employee forms?

- What type of leave polices do you have to comply with?

- Are you compliant with your city and state minimum wage?

Are your independent contractors truly independent?

Independent contractors are another major issue. When I talk about private practice, this is always one of the top concerns that I am very passionate about bringing to everyone's attention.

The Department of Labor has stated that more than 80 percent of independent contractors are misclassified. Are you ready to take that gamble? The fines from the IRS can extend to as high as $25,000 per misclassification with a lookback period of every independent contractor within three years of the investigation—even before factoring in past due wages. This can be easily a multi-million-dollar lawsuit waiting to happen.

Back in the day, my organization utilized independent contractors as the guidelines were different and more relaxed. All of our independent contractors fit the guidelines at the time in which they had their own business licenses. We had over eighty independent contractors that contributed to our workforce of over 350 clinicians, and I remember the day that Tom, our HR Director, came to me and told me we had to make a bold move; we needed to eliminate the utilization of independent contractors. I quickly jumped on board when I saw the changing tides of regulations and risk they posted for our organization.

The private practice community thought we were crazy when we made the changes to eliminate independent contractors from our practice. We offered each one a W-2 employee position, resulting in outrage from the independent contractors. They did not want to be employees because they wanted to continue to benefit from all their tax deductions. It was a bold move. At the end of the day, it was the best business move that we have ever made because we were able to mitigate a major risk that had the potential to close down our organization if we had not made it when we did.

It is a huge gamble to play fast and loose with these rules, so know what you are getting into. In 2018, the California Supreme Court made a ruling that makes it nearly impossible for employers to classify their workers as independent contractors. The unanimous decision has implications for the growing gig economy, such as Uber and Lyft, but it also extends to nearly every employment sector, especially healthcare.

Chief Justice Tani Cantil-Sakauye laid out three things a business must show for a worker to be classified as an independent contractor and they are:

1. The worker is free from the control and direction of the employer (*i.e. no training, no support, etc.*)

2. The worker performs work that is outside the hirer's core business (*i.e. how can a chiropractor office classify its chiropractors as 1099 contractors because they are part of the core business's offering?*)

3. The worker customarily engages in "an independently established trade, occupation, or business."

Although you may be thinking this is a California thing, it is not. I have seen more misclassification suits for my private practice clients in Texas than even in California. This is something every practice must keep in mind.

There are a few key points that the IRS will examine to begin with:

- How much control does the employer have over the workers' behavior and work results?

- Who controls the training?

- Where and what time does this person work?

When thinking about the proper classification of a 1099 Independent Contractor, you want to think about your landscaper, pool man, or jobs that are being delivered to multiple parties. The idea that a home health agency is utilizing 1099 contractors to deliver a core service within its business offer for a continuation of time is a major red flag and most likely a misclassification. These 1099 designations can raise major red flags. By and large, the IRS does not want to see a single funding source if someone is designated as a 1099, meaning that they want the independent contractor to deliver their specialized offering to multiple businesses.

If you've been working for one company for the last 10 years, and you are getting paid 40 hours a week as a 1099, you've likely been misclassified. Ten out of ten times you will lose—so just understand that. Please be advised that it is the responsibility of the "business" to prove that its staff are classified correctly. The business is the one that gets fined, not the 1099 independent contractor.

There are a number of common misnomers that I hear. I frequently hear one from speech language pathologists. They tell me, "Brandon, I have a full-time position with the school district. I only want 2-3 hours a week. Why can't I be an independent contractor?" That's a big flunk.

First of all, being an independent contractor has nothing to do with the amount of hours because you should have multiple funding sources. Any auditor will likely say, "Okay, you work two or three hours a week, that's a per diem W2 part time employee, not a contractor. Unless you have multiple companies that you are offering your service to." For example, Amber, the speech language pathologist would have a better chance of qualifying under the classification as an Independent Contractor if she has a business (LLC, PLLC, S-Corp) in which she provides her specialty to multiple business entities and has the ability to hire people under her to fulfill the job, control the timing when services are delivered, uses documentation with her letterhead, and invoices every entity.

Another statement that I frequently hear is, "Well, I was previously an independent contractor."

Well, that doesn't mean anything. What are you going to tell the DOL and the IRS if they come and audit your files? That the independent contractor told you they qualify because that was their classification for another agency?

"I want a per diem position." That's another statement that I frequently hear. The reality is that the terms "per diem" and "independent contractor" are different. You are a business owner. You are supporting multiple businesses not looking for a "per diem" position for side work. You are signing contracts. You can end that contract.

Overall, independent contractor classifications in your workforce are extremely risky for a private practice; therefore, I strongly recommend engaging the services of a consultant or labor attorney to break down if you are utilizing the proper classifications within your workforce.

HIPAA

I want you to understand that you should be training your team in this area. You should clearly articulate policies both in your employee packets and in your patient packets advising the risk and everything that falls under HIPAA. The HIPAA compliance and liability challenges are at an all-time high right now. I strongly recommend training your team and annually having them complete a test showcasing that they fully understand these provisions.

Start mentally preparing yourself now. When a HIPAA breach comes about, how do you respond? We unfortunately have experienced this nightmare scenario ourselves in our company with a HIPAA breach. We felt that we had done everything we could to prepare, and yet we still fell short. Given the rapid-moving world of cybersecurity and the increased attention being placed on privacy breaches, this is an area that you cannot neglect. Not only is it essential to do preventative measures, but it is also crucial to have strategies in place for when a breach occurs so that you can overcome it in a timely manner.

Work-Place Injury

One of the largest contributors to a potential lawsuit in private practices is when a proper work injury occurs. It is essential to train your staff on property work safety and to identify areas that could cause a work injury. Work injuries can happen during patient care, during remedial tasks, and even cleaning up a work station.

Recently, I had someone who was doing home health, and she just tripped on the street while walking to the patient's home. Her own negligence may have caused the injury—but she was on the job, placing me at the risk of negligence.

• • • • •

When it comes to meeting any of these requirements, take it slow and steady. If you ever have any doubt about if you are in compliance, do your homework and reach out to experts. It will be well worth the upfront investment of time and money to avoid hefty penalties down the line.

I share all of these compliance factors not to scare you, but to motivate you to prepare in advance and be aware of the risks so that you can mitigate them.

Remember the two necessary emotions I shared earlier—Love and Fear.

Love is what drives passion for what you do; Fear is what motivates you to prepare for the worst-case scenarios. One of my clients asked me the other day: "Brandon, how do you sleep at night based on all the compliance factors to be aware of?"

I said the way that I can get the best night's rest is knowing I am prepared for the worst-case scenario to the best of my ability. I look at what I can control and what I cannot control so that I can let go of the fear. I also run all the scenarios in a game I call "Private Practice Russian Roulette," in which I literally go through every risk factor and come up with how I would solve it if that factor occurred. Knowing our risks is one of the most essential recipes for success because it allows us to mitigate the occurrence. You may not be able to be the cause over everything, but if you create strategies for mitigation, you will limit your risk of being the "effect."

CHAPTER 4

Building a Business Plan

"Life is what happens to you while you're
busy making other plans."
—John Lennon

If there's any certainty in the world of business, it's that the pace of change will continue to accelerate. Every industry and sector is in the midst of profound digital disruption—particularly healthcare.

So how can you meaningfully prepare for the future given the rapid pace of technology and demographic changes? You might heed the words of President Dwight D. Eisenhower, who oversaw the D-Day invasion before he entered the White House. Ike famously said, "In preparing for battle I have always found that plans are useless, but planning is indispensable."

The Normandy invasion is remembered today as an iconic military victory and turning point in history, but it turned to a great degree on chance. The actual day of the invasion was rescheduled on more than one occasion due to the one element beyond even Eisenhower's control: the weather. With the wrong tide levels, the arriving Allied forces would have been sitting targets for the Nazis. Eisenhower ultimately recognized that a decision maker can only map out so many options but always remains at the mercy of chance to some degree.

However, even if the ultimate destination is impacted by forces beyond your control, you can still gain enormous value by simply undergoing the rigorous process of mapping out your strategy for the future.

Do I Really Need a Business Plan for My Private Practice?

Most likely, yes.

Despite the "move fast and break things" ethos that attracts many to entrepreneurship, there remains enormous value in clearly articulating your vision of the path forward.

There are a few key reasons to particularly remember when considering whether you should invest the time in a solid business plan for your practice.

- You are starting from scratch, with limited experience in running or growing a business.

- You own an established practice but need outside expertise to support sustained growth.

- You recognize that you need to better determine your specific objectives for the business.

- You need to raise money, whether in the form of fundraising, loans from the Small Business Administration, or venture capitalists.

A challenge for many health care professionals opening their own practice is that they are still novices to the world of business. Even after years of incredibly intensive training, education, or practicing medicine, most have simply not been formally exposed to the fundamentals of entrepreneurship.

Even with some of the world's most specialized expertise on health and medicine, you will likely struggle, at least initially, with some of the questions first year MBAs cover in their first semester. What's our unique value proposition? How do I fund my operation? What would be considered a healthy profit margin? What is the role of ethics as it relates to business decisions?

And what exactly goes into a business plan?

Some might be tempted to just launch into action and figure out the process of building a business along the way as they go—what we might call "building the airplane while flying it." Simply put, this is not the most effective or efficient approach. Those who typically follow this approach enjoy the instant gratification and typically the adrenaline of starting a new venture. That adrenaline will fuel them for about six to twelve months until either exhaustion or frustration or fear kicks in.

While there will inevitably be course corrections and reversals along the journey of building a private practice, a business plan is invaluable in ensuring that you begin on solid grounding. A well-constructed business plan helps ensure that you aren't just spinning your wheels but executing against a clearly drawn strategic roadmap that aligns with specific, measurable goals for your business. A quality business plan is also an invaluable tool in courting potential investors and demonstrating to them that you have clearly thought out an approach for maximizing usage of their funds.

Over the years, I have helped a number of practices through the process of developing the right plan. Sometimes established practices come to us seeking guidance on a potential pivot; more often, we find ourselves advising practices that have already launched but clearly need additional clarity around their business goals. It is clear that the practices that go on to thrive tend to be the ones that have invested time and energy up front considering where exactly they want to go from a business perspective.

In one of our first conversations, I always ask clients if they've written a formal business plan. I frequently find that they scoff at the question. "I'm not trying to get money," some reply—a bit indignant at the very notion.

My response is to ask them, "How do you know where you are going? What exactly are you trying to achieve?"

What I continually find is that the founder may very well have a fairly comprehensive notion of what success looks like in their head. It is very unlikely that they have taken the plunge to risk going into business for themselves without spending at least some time considering what victory will look like. However, they have never taken the time to translate that idea of success into a product that others can see—team members, investors, potential clients. Clinicians and healthcare providers are often so invested in their own passion for their work that they forget one of the first rules we learn in elementary school math class: "Show your work!"

When we can clearly write out and document our vision, suddenly it's no longer just a vision in our head. It is a blueprint, a road map, one that others can follow.

What Should Go into Your Business Plan?

Thanks to technology, it is easier than ever to gain a sense of what a professional business plan should look like with just a few keystrokes. There can be so much information, in fact, that it can be overwhelming to determine what format is most appropriate for your practice's business plan.

The reality is that there are many models that may be appropriate depending on a number of variables. Below I'll present one model for a plan that may fit your needs—but it is just one example. There is no one-size-fits-all approach. This chapter will go on to provide additional reference points and resources for writing effective business plans. More than becoming too hung up on the specifics of any particular model, you should focus on the larger principle at play here—ensuring that you have carefully thought through your plan of attack early in the process of establishing your own practice.

Below are some of the key sections that you will likely want to ensure are reflected in your business plan.

Section 1 - Executive Summary

Your plan should likely begin with a concise description designed to fit the limited time of prospective investors. This section provides an overall snapshot of your business plan, outlining the contours of your vision and overall business strategy.

You might think of this section as a chance to clearly define your mission statement: What drove you to establish your practice? What challenges are you seeking to address with your expertise? Who are the key founders and what role will they play? How do you plan to position your products and services within the broader, existing marketplace?

This section would include such components as:

- The Mission Statement

- Essential Company Information (when your business was formed, name of founders and their roles, any additional info on number of employees, locations, etc.)

- Growth Highlights / Goals

- Your Products / Services

- Summary of Opportunity

Section 2 - Company Description

In this section, you establish what services your company will offer and your unique value proposition. What expertise or assets do you bring to the market that aren't currently being met by existing competitors? What market is your business serving?

This is an area where you especially need to be considering the vantage point of an investor with no shortage of options for directing their funds. They will seek to clearly understand what competitive advantage you can bring to your customers.

In summary, this section would include:

- Description of the nature of your business. List the marketplace needs that you seek to satisfy.

- Explanation of how your products and services meet these needs.

- List of the specific consumers, organizations or businesses that your company serves or will serve.

- Explanation of the competitive advantages that you believe will make your business a success such as your location, expert personnel, efficient operations, or ability to bring value to your customers.

Section 3 - Market Analysis

This is an area where I have often found clients especially need to invest significant time; over time, it can dramatically help your marketing and overall strategic growth if you have clearly outlined the landscape for your industry. What is currently happening in the market? How is federal healthcare policy reform and all of its ongoing implications likely to affect your business?

As an example, many Americans continue to struggle with high premiums and expenses associated with healthcare across the board. This will surely remain a hot topic for investors as more experts in the field consider how the existing system can be disrupted to better meet the consumer demands of the 21st century. Speaking directly to these concerns in your market analysis will only help demonstrate what role your business can play in the ongoing work of modernizing the U.S. healthcare system. How exactly will your business streamline and support the needs of your customers?

Include as much information on your target market as possible. I was recently meeting with investors who asked me about the size of the market for a particular business.

As I broke down the size of the potential pool of customers to the investor group, I was reminded of how relatively small a pool it was considering the big scheme of things—after all, nearly every American will interact with the healthcare industry at some point in their lives. I went on to explain how I was going to scale the business given a relatively small market share based on our specialty.

Your market analysis might also touch on areas such as:

- Pricing and gross margin targets

- Competitor analysis

- SWOT (Strengths, Weaknesses, Opportunities, Threats) Analysis

- Potential barriers to market

- Industry description and outlook

- Information about your target market

- Distinguishing characteristics

- Size of primary target market

- How much market share can you gain?

- How important is your target market to your competitors?

- What is your window of opportunities?

- Regulatory restrictions (think any regulatory requirements such as home health licensure, etc.)

Section 4 - Organization of Management

At the end of the day, your business is about the people behind it. That remains true even in an age of technology saturation in every part of our lives. Anyone that you are showing this business plan to, whether it be strategic partners or investors, will want to clearly understand the dynamics of your team and the expertise they bring to the table. How will you organize their ownership and involvement? What is their track record in the field? What unique skills and education do they bring to the endeavor?

There have been times when I largely lean on my own experience in pitches when discussing the organizational leadership side of the business. Then there are times when I recognize that I need to highlight the full breadth of the team I have assembled, highlighting the experience of the executive team or board of directors that I have helped put together. I typically focus on the broader team when I see a need to show that we bring a diversified skill set to the table.

In summary, this section would likely include:

- Ownership details (percentage of ownership, involvement, etc.).

- Details on the track record and history of success for ownership and management team

- Details on education, special skills, unique experience of management team and ownership

- Board of Director Information (where applicable)

- Type of legal structure

Organizational Board Structure

By thinking through what type of structure is optimal for the leadership of your organization, you can clearly define lines of authority and who is responsible for what functions.

Org Chart
Sound of Music Home Health, Inc.

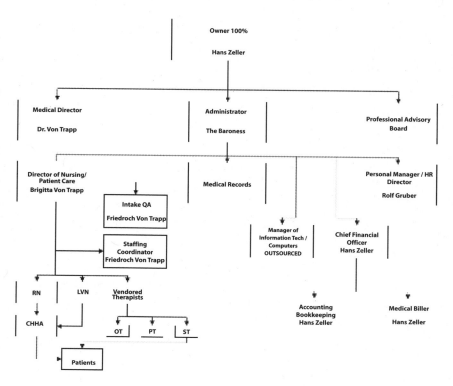

At their heart, organizational charts are really about establishing accountability. I often use the sample seen here that reflects what the leadership structure might look like for the Von Trapp family in *The Sound of Music* if they were a home health agency—just underscoring that every organization of every stripe needs to develop some kind of formal structure in order to function well (as you can see in the collapse of some organizations that follow a model of leader-less authority, like the activist Occupy Wall Street movement). There are some highly innovative organizations in Silicon Valley that have found some success with decentralized models of authority, but they generally have already built very robust innovation ecosystems in which self-organizing principles are embedded culturally within the fabric of the organization itself. For the vast majority of private practices, it will be far easier to opt for a more conventional hierarchy with clear lines of accountability and decision-making authority.

This really amounts to Business 101. We want to identify who's in your organization. We want to identify who they report to and what their role is. Ultimately, we want to also understand how their role contributes to the value proposition of the entire organization so that they have "buy in" for what they do on a daily basis.

Legal Business Structures

There are several options when it comes to your legal business structure. I highly recommend that you consult with your attorney and CPA as they have both legal repercussions and tax repercussion. Here are some key business structures to keep in mind:

Sole Proprietorships – A sole proprietorship is the simplest business form under which one can operate a business. The sole proprietorship is not a legal entity. It simply refers to a person who owns the business and is personally responsible for its debts. It is an unincorporated business owned and run by one individual with no distinction between the business and you.

Cooperative – A cooperative is a business or organization owned by and operated for the benefit of those using its services. Profits and earning generated by the cooperative are distributed among the members, also known as user-owners. Typically an elected board of directors and officers runs the cooperative while regular members have the voting power to control the direction of the cooperative. For example, "Ocean Spray" has an agricultural cooperative of growers of cranberries and grapefruit. It currently has over 700 member growers.

General Partnership (GP) – These are general partnerships in which profits, liability, and management duties are divided equally among partners.

Limited Partnership (LP) – These are more complex than general partnerships. Limited partnerships allow partners to have limited liability as well as limited input with management decisions. Limited Partnerships are attractive to investors of short-term projects.

Joint Venture (JV) – Joint ventures act as a general partnership, but for only a limited period or for a single project. They can be extended but must be documented appropriately.

The majority of readers of this book will likely be organized into one type of corporation. Again, there are a few options here:

- Nonprofit Corporation: An incorporated entity designed to perform activities and enter transactions without the intent of "generating customary profits." A nonprofit can show "profit, but it must be reinvested into the organization. Please note that receiving 501(C) (3) status is a separate process than being incorporated as a nonprofit organization. 501 (C) (3) status is the process of becoming recognized as a federally tax-exempt charity that does not pay income or sales tax and allows donors to write off donations.

- C-Corporation: The standard "C" corporation is a separate legal entity owned by shareholders. The corporate structure limits each owner's (shareholder's) personal liability for the corporation's business debts to the amount invested in the company by the shareholder.

- S-Corporation: An S-corporation is a standard corporation that has elected a special tax status with the IRS. The formation requirements are the same as those for C corporations. (Incorporation documents must be filed with the state.) The S corporation's special tax status eliminates the double taxation that can occur with a C corporation's income. Any tax due is paid by shareholders at their individual tax rates.

- Limited Liability Company (LLC): Viewed as a hybrid between corporation and partnership. LLC is formed under state law and gives you personal liability protection. Tax-wise, an LLC is similar to an S corporation. Please also be advised that many of you may choose a (PLLC), which stands for a Professional Limited Liability Company. Often physical therapists, speech language pathologists, and occupational therapists will classify their business as a Professional Limited Liability Company.

Section 5 - Service or Product Line

The next part of your business plan touches on your service and product line.

Consider questions such as:

- How does your service benefit your community?

- Exactly what's your differentiation from your competitors?

- Is there intellectual property? Is there something you are doing that no one else is doing?

- What are your research and development activities?

Section 6 - Marketing Sales

It's critical that you fully examine your marketing strategy for your business. This should be an ongoing business evaluation process unique to your company. I am a big believer that strategic relationships are everything. I used to knock on the doors of 50 doctors a week to create my referral network. Every lunch I went to and every call that I made was fundamentally about building relationships that could support my ultimate vision for the company.

There is no single way to approach a marketing strategy. It should be an ongoing business evaluation process and unique to your company.

All of the following should be reflected in your strategy:

- Market penetration strategy

- Growth strategy

- Channels of distribution strategy

- Communication strategy

- Sales strategies and activities

Financial Projections

This may be the aspect of your plan that strikes the most fear in your heart, but it is necessary. After you have analyzed the market and set clear objectives for your business, you must develop financial projections to highlight your expected trajectory for investors and other stakeholders or even for your own strategic record.

Your financial analysis should include, but not be limited to, these components:

- Financial trend analysis

- Financial projections

- Historical Financial Data

- Projected cash flow analysis

- Profitability study

This is the area of your plan where metrics are everything. How many clients are you planning to target in the first month? 100 perhaps? Okay. How are we going to get there? What's the revenue look like? What's your gross revenue? What's your cash flow? Is it going to take time to get paid? Keep in mind that insurance is a slower payer source. All of these factors must be accounted for. Please keep in mind that this section is so helpful in identifying if you have an optimum business model. I typically start all my consulting relationships with an analysis of their financial condition and projections because it helps us identify if the business model is optimized for success.

Scalability

This is one of the final factors for us to review. In simplest terms, scalability is equivalent to growth.

When I launch a company, I usually launch a company with the understanding of where I am going to start and where it's going to go. Assuming that I grow it to a point where it's ready for scalability, the right partner can come in and take it to that next level.

The right scalability for your business will depend largely on your ambitions and what you want to gain from the venture. Some of you might want smaller scalability in accordance with more modest goals—some of you may want to build an empire. Regardless of your vision, there are plenty of tools available online as well as consultants that are here to help you get started.

Additional Resources for Creating an Effective Business Plan

- Business Plan Templates:

http://www.bplans.com

- U.S. Small Business Administration:

www.sba.gov

- Sample of Kinesio Physical Therapy Business Plan:

http://kskjoldspt.weebly.com/uploads/3/0 /9/0/30903037/ business_plan_final.pdf

- SCORE Business Plan Template:

https://www.score.org/resource/businessplan-template-startup-business

◆━━━━━━◆✕◆━━━━━━◆

CHAPTER 5

Developing a Bulletproof Business Foundation

"Castles made of sand, fall in the sea, eventually."
—Jimi Hendrix

One of the most well-known biblical parables comes from the book of Matthew. During the Sermon on the Mount, Jesus tells his followers a story of two men—one who built his house upon a foundation of rock and one who built on sand.

The house built upon rock is ready to withstand the ravages when a storm finally comes. The builder was wise to choose his foundation carefully.

There's probably no surprise at what happened to the house built on sand—it collapses in the storm.

Religion aside, the lesson here is clear—take great care that the foundation you build upon can withstand the storms of life. This is of great relevance for us as we head into this chapter. Now that you have written your business plan, it's time for the next step—developing a business foundation that is truly bulletproof.

What exactly do we mean by the foundation?

It may be helpful to think of your house. Would you be enthusiastic about building a house on sinking mud? Not likely—you want your structure to last and it clearly would not if built on sinking mud. One of the best investments an entrepreneur can make is investing in the foundation of his or her business, which typically starts with a thorough evaluation of the business model.

You don't just build a foundation for today's needs, but for the future. When we first started our private practice, it was truly a two-person affair. Over the next decade, it grew into 10 full-time staff. The nature of the foundation began to shift. The proverbial house began to sink in a little.

We came in and actually reassessed the foundation from top to bottom, building a completely new infrastructure that would not only support the nine employees we had, but could ultimately support future growth. It had to be a foundation that could pivot with change, because change is a major component of the business process. Over the course of time, our foundation strengthened and evolved which allowed us to grow effectively and efficiently in staff, in revenue, and in service offering.

What we have to do is We have to come in and actually reassess the foundation, build a whole infrastructure, so that you are not just supporting your nine employees of today, but a big enough foundation that will allow you to pivot as time passes.

Take a look at the diagram pictured below from the writer Steven Fisher.

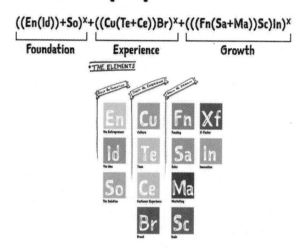

The diagram illustrates an important equation—foundation plus experience equals growth. This is a very important concept to keep in mind. It is relevant to all of us as entrepreneurs.

You all are in business for yourself because you have a solution. That's your foundation.

It falls upon all of us to craft the full experience: your team, your culture, your customer experience, your brand—everything.

Let's take one of the most famous businesses and consider this approach from their example.

Apple started with the foundation of an idea, a solution, and an entrepreneur—and it actually failed at first. It wasn't until Steve Jobs had left the company, matured, and returned—fully in control of his abilities—that his team was able to craft a world-class experience in which everything started to click-team, culture, customer experience, brand.

Suddenly your personal favorite products were from Apple—the iPhone, the iPod, whatever you prefer. In every case, the true success of that product lies in the experience that the company has created for the user. Prior to Apple, it was very rare for anyone to truly enjoy the experience of interacting with their computer. Steve Jobs' central insight was that customers would pay a healthy premium for the privilege of spending time with devices that they actually enjoyed using.

When I met my wife, funnily enough, her father had a rule that they weren't allowed to have Apple products. He was very much of an "old school" mentality when it came to his technology choices. He was very loyal to his MP3 player, for example. He actually had built PCs for a living, instilling a high sense of loyalty to what was very likely an inferior product, in my personal opinion.

So he was a no-Apple man. As a result, my wife had never used an iPad or iPod. I decided that I was going to truly break the mold with her family by proposing to her on an iPod -and sure enough I did! I engraved it later with the date, and she finally got her first iPod—her first Apple product ever.

Cut forward to today—his daughter-in-law works for Apple and his whole family has Apple products. It is quite a sea of change from the old way he ran the household.

I share this with you to highlight what Apple did. They crafted a great user experience—what it feels like, what it tastes like, what the team is like. When you walk into an Apple store, you know without looking at any sign, exactly where you are. You can't tell me that there's another company that has built an experience like this. When I survey Apple employees, which I've been so fortunate to be able to do, they tell me that there's no other company they want to work for. Why? The experience and the team that Apple has created is not available anywhere else is what they tell me. If you ever have an opportunity to tour a corporate office for Apple, I recommend exploring both their work stations as well as their culture offerings such as healthcare services, cafeteria, and how they create an empowering environment that ultimately delivers on quality and efficiency.

One of the last things that I want you to keep in mind when evaluating your foundation is the analysis of your business model. I think it is essential that you look at the business model as the foundation of which your business grows and opportunity of reaching optimum success. I recently had a consultation with an aesthetician whose private practice specializes in skin and beauty care. She shared with me that she is a "one-woman shop"; however, she recently diversified her offerings and took on the lease of another office next-door to focus on permanent makeup through tattooing.

The first thing I asked is if she had plans to hire or bring in outside specialists for either the "skin-care" or "permanent make-up care." She said no. I then asked if she could have done both skin care and permanent makeup under one single office, and she shared that she could not at this time due to space requirements and equipment.

My next question was: "Why did you decide to diversify your services? Were you not busy enough under the 'skin-care' services?" She shared that she was drawn to the art of "permanent makeup" and wanted to diversify her offering. I then mentioned that she had one major flaw in her business model based on her current goals. The major business flaw was that she opened two offices (i.e. fixed expenses) that were both based on one person's time because she was not willing to consider bringing on more staff. The result is a limit to the ROI on her fixed expenses; she would essentially be stealing potential from one business to service the other.

Ultimately, her downfall in her foundation and business model is that there is no scalability as long as everything is tied to her manpower. She invested a lot in adding new equipment and office space. Her return on investment, however, was less than she was making on her "skin-care/beauty-care" services. In practice, she invested in a hobby instead of expanding the strength of her business foundation by providing more financial upside.

Growing the Dream

So we build the foundation, we craft the experience, and then we grow the dream. The dream is about taking the foundation and the experience—bringing about funding, sales, marketing, scale, your ex-factor, and innovation.

And yes, in healthcare today, we have to be investors. Look at any practice that you have been to recently and ask yourself what makes them successful. The two aspects that I find are usually the experience and the innovation—bottom line.

So as we build your startup, as we remodel your startup, let's get the foundation set up. Let's craft your experience. And let's grow the dream.

Building the Optimal Business Foundation

I have four components for an optimal business foundation. This is what I focus on when I am remodeling or building a new business or an existing business that needs remodeling. I always need structure in systems. I need a winning team. I need an optimum payer mix and strong consumer outcomes.

If your clients aren't winning, you won't win—bottom line. Ensure that these four things are in place and truly nothing can stop you.

The Fear Factor

I want to talk a little bit about this fear factor because every private practice-preneur that I have ever met has fear. Most of them come to me because they are not achieving the success they want to. The issue is not that they are not successful—the issue is that they feel they could be attaining more success, but they have hit a roadblock.

When I take a hard look, I often find that they are blocked by fear. That is the roadblock. So, one of the things we do is break down that fear. I explain to clients that fear can be their biggest asset when it's channeled appropriately. Those that don't have fear often

THE PRIVATE PRACTICE SURVIVAL GUIDE

fail. And that's something that gets missed. They tell me, "What do you mean, those who don't have fear fail?" Those who don't have fear often make mistakes. They are the equivalent of a car going 200 miles an hour with no safety precautions.

I want you to channel fear as a tool for success by confronting it head-on. What exactly is the fear that is stopping you from doing something? Whatever that fear looks like, I want you to look at it straight in the eyes, and then I want you to ask yourself—why am I reacting this way? How can I overcome this fear? How can I utilize this fear to make it my most successful action in my business?

Remember earlier when I referenced "The Private Practice Russian Roulette" strategy? Develop your worst case scenario list. This is something that I do this with my clients all the time. It is a helpful exercise to ask yourself every now and then—just what am I so afraid of? What is the worst that can happen? How can I prevent it? How can I overcome it if it occurs?

For me, my absolute worst-case scenario is that I have a client's practice not reach optimum success on my watch. That's an important fear for my consulting practice.

Then I ask myself, "What are you doing about it? Is the fear going to keep the practice alive and thriving?"

No.

I need to utilize my fear in a productive way. I need to use that fear as fuel for my hustle.

Every day I am asked, "How do you do what you do?" And I give a simple answer in return: I hustle. The fear is what keeps pushing me to push myself to the next level. I won't let myself get complacent. What's my fear? The fear that all of it will disappear tomorrow.

Should that happen, my response would be to keep creating and keep moving forward. Every successful entrepreneur that I've ever met has utilized fear as the form to hustle. Push yourself to be great. Don't settle. Mediocrity is what ultimately kills so many businesses. Be great, not good. Don't let your fear be the barrier to success. Use your fear to motivate you to attain even greater success.

I want to highlight two tools in particular that are important in the self-discovery phase.

One is SWOT analysis, which we briefly covered earlier. This is something that is used in every business. It is most certainly a concept straight out of Business 101, but it's very effective.

Use it to break down the strengths of your business. These strengths might include your internal measures, your team, your education, your experience, your funding. It should include everything internal about you that's strong.

I want you to keep looking internally. I also want you to look at your weaknesses. Where are you weak? Is it in your systems? Is it your IQ? Is it not knowing what you do or don't know? What are the things internally that you evaluate your business as weak in?

Let's now switch our perspective to the external factors. The next thing we are looking at is opportunity. Step out that door of your business. What are the opportunities?

What can you achieve that is laying at the horizon? Whether your organization is service model, technology model, delivery model, quality model, what's the opportunity that's at that horizon? Name it and seize it.

The last component of a SWOT analysis is very important. Look around, scan left to right—what are the threats? Who's around you? What's around you? What's playing a part? Is there a political scene influencing your market that could be a threat? What are the factors outside your business that are a threat that could influence its success?

Goals

Now that you have conducted your SWOT analysis, it's time to pinpoint some of your goals. I like to establish "smart goals." Be as specific as possible with your goals—think through your "who, what, where, when, why, which." Outline all of the specifics. You should be able to tell yourself how your goals are measurable, which results in accountability. Where are you going? What's the measurable metric that will tell you when you have arrived at your goal?

I want you to ask yourself a hard question—is it truly attainable? And when it's attainable, is it easily attainable or more difficult?

Your long-term goals can be harder, but you want to have some short-term success. Therefore, it is essential to measure the attainability of your goal.

You also must assess the relevance of your goal. Is this goal worthwhile? Is it going to get you to the next level of success?

The last factor to consider is time—when? Your objective should include a time limit. When are you going to achieve that goal?

Here is a diagram as a reminder:

(Source: http://habitica.wikia.com/wiki/SMART_Goal_Setting)

You now have your SWOT analysis conducted and your smart goals ready to go.

The Secrets to Success in the 21st Century

I have to tell you there's one thing that is changing the landscape of business and private practice in today's environment, and that's efficiency. That is the key.

When I go into any new businesses, I measure efficiency as a key metric. Many look at efficiency in different ways. I am not telling you to slash your workforce costs down to the bone and replace everyone with robots. I don't think that's an optimal strategy.

But you have to be able to evaluate how long something takes and the return on investment of the time, as well as if it can be done more effectively and faster. Efficiency in operations can greatly empower quality, effectiveness via time management, and prioritization of patient care. Efficiency saves private practice owners money and streamlines the bottom line while increasing quality of time.

To be clear, I am not trying to free up your time so you can go on vacation to your private island. I am trying to free up your time so you can do what you do well. Efficiency often increases consistency and continuity from an operational standpoint.

I have encountered plenty of efficiency nightmares in my time. For one example, I would point to the reality. 40 to 50 percent of the private practices that I visit clearly have major challenges with their efficiency.

I will go speak to whoever is running the show—the owner or the office manager, perhaps. I will ask them to show me their data. What they often end up doing is pulling out a three-ring binder that consists of more than 1,000 pages. They lay it down on the desk, and I almost want to faint when I see the size of it.

I ask them, "What exactly is this?"

They proudly reply, "Everything."

When I ask them to clarify what exactly constitutes "everything," they inform me that this binder is comprised of their ledger, their patient information, and everything they need organized into one file.

I invariably start laughing. They reply, "What's so funny?"

"How confident are you with a computer?" I ask. "Because you are about to become much more confident after I lay out some of the potential scenarios that could bring harm to your business."

What happens if an employee steals that from you—what are you going to do?

What happens if your building burns down?

How fast can you get me data from it and how long does it take you to log in?

Those binders are no longer valid in today's environment. Today we live in a digital world. We have electronic medical records, QuickBooks, customer retention software, marketing software, and bank statements. You can upload checks to your bank account with an app, and they will be deposited in your account the very next day.

In this day and age, you simply can't rely on a rusty old binder. You need to be leveraging every digital tool at your disposal.

I've seen similar old school technology being used in payments in which practices were using antiquated card swiping machines to accept credit cards. Instead of allowing customers to swipe their credit card quickly, staff were required to type in all of the information from the card into the machine. Then the information from the card would be kept in a physical binder—a clear violation of laws, which require this information to be maintained with proper encryption. I unfortunately see these gross violations often.

The same organizations may then be relying on sending out invoices and bills via the mail, to the tune of hundreds being sent out each week. Processes like this are a major waste of time and resources, draining energy that your staff could be using to far more productive ends. I told one of these clients about a modernized merchant services system—all digital, all information conducted via email, everything fully HIPPA compliant. My client could now push a button to deliver invoices, receipts, and super bills where before she had been bogged down in hours upon hours of tedious homework.

She told me, "Brandon, you literally just took 75 percent of my day away."

I said, "Great, what's next? What can we put on you? Let's use your brain instead of your body."

I am a big believer in utilizing the mentality of working smarter not harder, which often results in using your brain before your body. Otherwise, you are going to end up getting replaced by computers.

I hate to tell you that, but that is what is increasingly happening in the world today. Go to the United Terminal at Newark Airport and you will see what I am talking about. In this day and age, just about any task that is focused on routine procedures can be replicated and likely performed much better by technology.

Where we as humans still have a competitive advantage is in the higher level critical thinking skills that machines still can't match—at least, not yet. We need to focus more of our attention on bigger picture, strategic thinking and delegate more of the routine processes to technology.

The piles of filing, the credit card machines, the binders, the old school scheduling books—they are all going away. And good riddance, for the most part. Like Bob Dylan at the Newport Folk Festival in 1965, we are going electric.

It is the solution, whether you love it or hate it. My advice is to embrace it as it simply is a necessity in today's environment. So we need to select the right systems for you. Each client is different. I've implemented now multiple electronic medical record systems, practice management systems, human resource systems, payroll systems, and marketing systems. I've done it all. And not all of them are right for everyone. So we have to look at what are those pieces that are essential to you.

The key to selecting the right systems is ensuring it saves you time. Just because it has all the bells and whistles, It doesn't mean that it's right for you.

I'm reminded of a story about when my father-in-law called me in. He had just gotten himself this brand new car, and he was very excited. He had been driving it for about three weeks at this point.

I said, "How's the car?"

He said, "Oh, it is okay."

I said, "What do you mean it's okay? It sounds amazing. It's got everything."

He replied, "That's the problem Brandon. I don't know how to use all the bells and whistles."

My statement to him is either you have to learn it or you shouldn't have bought all the bells and whistles. So you are only as good as your ability to utilize your system.

The same is true in our business. I find that the world of operating and picking the pieces does not always take into account finding the right fit for your business. I want the value. I want the bells and whistles. But sometimes you've got to find the happy medium.

The key to effective systems is understanding the following factors. What's the problem that you are trying to solve? What's the frequency of the problem? This is really important. I hear it all the time when people say to me, "Well, you know, once in a while this happens."

I reply, "I don't want to know once in a while; I want to know how quickly it occurs. Because the more frequent the occurrence, the more valuable the system is." If it happens once in a blue moon, we are not buying systems for that right now.

Time saving is a very important factor to consider. What's the return on investment of that solution? What's the scalability based on the idea? I just recently implemented a new electronic medical records program in my practice. The reason why I picked it was the scalability. It was able to support growth without it costing too much money: That initial investment proved to be quite worthwhile; whereas some people need a different system because they don't need that same scalability.

All of these are the factors that can help you decide on an acquisition, but you need to be looking at these pieces when you are evaluating your systems.

There are many examples of technical solutions to consider for private practice systems. These range from electronic medical records to practice management platform.

You need to brush up on the full spectrum of technology options—cloud-based storage servers, patient portal platforms for all of your forms that go to the patients, automated marketing tools, Telehealth platforms, and automated communication tools like Mail Chimp.

Regardless of the tool you select, it's fundamentally only as good as the problem it's solving for you and the time that it's saving.

Understanding the Mind, the Body, and Spirit Phenomena in Building Your Staff

This issue of quality of life and wellness is very, very important. We all eat, sleep, and breathe each day. No matter how hard we push ourselves and how much drive we bring to our work, we only have so much gas in the tank. Without regular and ongoing rejuvenation, we not only will be no good for ourselves, but we will be no good for our businesses or our customers.

As I mentioned earlier, in today's digitized economy, we need to be replacing our bodies with our minds. We need to focus on where we can add the greatest value and not bog all of our energy down in endless tedium that can be better handled by bots and technology.

When we try to do too much, we drain ourselves of our energy—our most important and precious resource. We need to not only be thoughtful and intentional about where we spend our energy during the work day, we also need to be sure to take good physical care of ourselves. The same is very much true of our employees.

I have found that the more body and spirit I have, the more efficient I begin to become. I find that I am creating solutions to make my mind more or my body more effective.

Let's talk about the body. Of course you are very invested in your company and your vision. You have a vested interest in meeting your goals and living up to your full potential. But the same cannot always be said for each and every person on your staff. The reality is that for many people, their job will just be a job. I am sure you have seen this reflected at your organization, or perhaps at another business you patronize. The employee follows directions, but there's no visible sign of a proactive effort in identifying problems.

This employee could literally walk off a bridge into the deep end of the ocean if you told them to because they are not thinking with the job. Every day I challenge my people to adopt the mindset of an owner. I tell them, "You are a decision-maker. You might not be the business owner, but you are empowered to come to me with a solution. If you are just sitting back and documenting your clinical notes the same way and you are not elevating problems to me, then you are not fully doing your job. You are not fulfilling your true potential, and you are not taking ownership of the business."

That proactive mindset is essential in today's success. I find real concern when individuals are not bought into our mission. When I go audit a practice, I can typically identify fairly quickly who are the bodies—the ones just sleepwalking through the motions—and who are the leaders who are thinking about challenges from the perspective of a business owner.

I hear the same unfortunate story from so many business owners.

They tell me some variation on the following: "Brandon, the reason why I am hitting my head against the wall is I have to do everything for them. I literally have to tie their shoes—it feels like that anyway. What exactly am I them paying for?"

My statement to them is, "You should no longer be paying for bodies. Bodies will be replaced by technology."

You already see this at fast food joints. McDonald's and Shake Shack increasingly are transitioning from a model in which a flesh-and-blood person asks for your order; the entire process is switching to one that is dominated by touch screens.

The simple reality is that to get ahead in the 21st century, we all must be able to think deeply and contribute value to an organization beyond simply following directions.

In short, you must empower your employees to not only be the body, but to also be the spirit and the mind so that they can contribute to your organization on a greater level.

Otherwise many functions can simply be replaced with computers. It's not a pleasant thing to eliminate a job—many of us first got into entrepreneurship because we liked the idea of creating jobs. But the technology trend lines are clear. Filing will soon be an antiquated practice, along with faxing. Services must become more streamlined across the board to meet much more robust customer demands. That means your employees will need to be contributing much more in the day-to-day operations than simply pushing buttons or following directions.

When you do have employees who proactively think outside of their narrow role and identify bigger challenges or opportunities, make sure that you truly cherish them. They have given you a sign that they are hungry for more responsibility and more personal agency—so give it to them! Let them take on greater responsibility for their role and contribute to the organization.

Let others see that the way to advance in your operation is to work smarter, not simply harder. Congratulate staff members who find ways to free up their time and carry out their work more efficiently. Such employees are always on the lookout for ways to add value to the company.

I've known some managers who take a much dimmer view of employees behaving in the way they have described. They have a much more "old school" attitude of what is expected. They may even be threatened by a staff member voluntarily taking on more responsibility. Don't make this same mistake—the reality is that most talented people are going to be ambitious. You need to give them the space to grow and try on new hats; otherwise, you will find yourself losing them to competitors in your space. As the old saying goes, "Help them grow or watch them go."

I am personally very proud of the core team that I have built.

This is most certainly not any roster of bodies. My team is comprised of people who are all mind, body, and spirits. I could not achieve a fraction of what I am able to get done each day if I did not have them in my corner backing me up each step of the way.

You likely have a good conception by now of what goes into the body aspect of this trifecta. How about the spirit?

I would define it as the ability to harness your energy to productive means. When your employees live your mission in their spirit, they truly eat, sleep, and breathe what they are doing each day. They come to work each day with an ownership level that would make you think that it is their name on the door outside.

I have brought in receptionists who truly embody this concept. It can happen with anyone at any level of your organization. There's a famous story about a construction site where three men were laboring away. A man came upon the site and asked each of them, "What are you doing here?"

One man replied, "I'm laying bricks."

The second man answered, "I'm building a wall."

And the third replied, "I'm building a cathedral!"

No prizes for guessing which of the three men was bringing his full spirit to work—and no prizes for guessing which was likely the most productive. It is far easier to work with a sense of joy when you firmly believe in the ultimate goal that you are striving toward.

I saw this ethos with some of my receptionists. They don't just answer the phone because it's ringing, and they have to pick it up. They answer the phone with an expectant tone as though they fully expect to change the life of the other person on the line.

They are not just doing it because it is part of the job; they are doing it because they have passion.

These employees have the highest level of ownership in this stake. They constantly seek ways to contribute and become the office superheroes. They are able to confront recommendations as well as make corrections. From their viewpoint—if they contribute on the greatest level to the company, the company will contribute and impact their own lives. The overall exchange will be at the highest level—beyond just compensation, inspiring employees to feel they are a part of something greater.

I have three employees that illustrate this.

I will tell you that two of them are unfortunately no longer with the company. Why is that? They just didn't grow in the way we needed—not in mind, body, or spirit.

The first was a front desk person at our clinic. She literally fell asleep on the job.

How do you fall asleep at the front desk job? She simply had no motivation when there wasn't a supervisor looking over her shoulder.

She did try to cultivate an image. She was very enthusiastic when I was around, conveying the brand of a dream employee. But at the end of the day, she was a body. She only worked as hard as someone watching her. She only did what she was told. Ultimately that position got eliminated. I was able to utilize technology to replace many aspects of her position and bring in the next level of person at a higher level to contribute much more.

The second person was a little disconnected, but she was able to bring solutions, and that was important. But ultimately what I found was that she never was able to get fully behind our mission and invested. At the end of the day, she truly did have an attitude of clocking in and clocking out.

As for the last employee—she transformed my company. She brings me ideas and critiques me. She actually tells me, "Brandon, I think you could do this better." And I can hear it from her because I know she has my best interest at hand.

I believe she is still fulfilled as well. The idea that she can critique her boss is so empowering. I value her input. She has grown in eight years with me and has become an invaluable member of the team.

I can call on her. I can trust in her. I have eyes, ears, mind, body, spirit with me in this march.

It all comes down to a unified team at the end of the day. So as you build your workforce, realize that workforce and that investment in workforce is only as good as your weakest link. And the more you can streamline your operations and bring greater effectiveness, the more you can afford to bring in the mind, body, and spirit.

—◆—✕—◆—

CHAPTER 6

Making Your Metrics Matter

"There are three kinds of lies: lies, damned lies, and statistics."
—British Prime Minister Benjamin Disraeli

Now that we've built your foundation, we need to hold it accountable and that means making your metrics matter. It has been said. That numbers don't lie, but they can most certainly tell us a very different story depending on the question that you ask.

We hear an awful lot of discussion these days about the power of big data, but why precisely do metrics matter so much anyway? Because they provide a measurement tool for accountability. They provide a reference point for the direction your private practice is going. The metrics that you implement should increase efficiency and effectiveness. They should be the guiding light—the GPS for achieving your private practice goals.

That is why they matter. Ultimately, I want you to think of metrics as your best friend. When I go into practices on a daily basis, I ask the team, "What are the metrics that you use?"

Many of them reply something to the effect of, "I don't know. What are metrics?"

That is about the time that I realize that I have more work to do than I anticipated!

We're going to shed some light on a few key metrics. One of the common themes I have found with many entrepreneurs—especially when this private practice is their baby—is that they tend to micromanage their team. In my opinion, metrics are what separate the micromanagers from the effective managers. They are the reason that you can empower your team to buy-in, take investment in the numbers, and be held accountable without requiring a supervisor to watch over their shoulder at everything they do.

There are two areas of metrics that are especially important for you to understand, especially in the healthcare field in which so many businesses use service-based models. I am referring to the difference between variable expenses and fixed expenses. Not understanding the nuances of the differences here can be a major mistake that will cost quite a bit of money.

For some clarification, a variable expense is one that changes—fixed does not. Simple enough, right?

I have tried to tie my therapist compensation as much as possible to variable expenses to ensure a greater return on investment and to serve as a strong performance incentive. For example, if I pay a staffer more when they complete 75 percent completion, it's a win-win for everyone involved. But what if your productivity metrics begin to decline? What can you do then to turn the ship around?

That is likely the time to turn your attention to your fixed expenses—these might include such measures as insurance and administrative staff. I try as much as possible to limit my fixed expenses so that all of my staff members can be rewarded consummate with the company's overall growth and bottom line. I know that my team is only as strong as the individuals within in it.

There are some key metrics in particular that I want you to keep in mind. Statistics and metrics can be thought of a bit like a GPS for your organization.

My clients literally live off statistics. They serve as a roadmap to hold everyone accountable. I maintain metrics even for the return on investment that I offer my clients to ensure that I have a very clear vision of where they are headed. These are broken down to a very granular level, to include daily, weekly, monthly, quarterly, and annual statistics.

Some statistics that you might look at could include the productivity of each clinician, their daily and monthly averages, how much they are billing—all of these measures help you to evaluate the value they are delivering.

The productivity of my administrative staff is another measure. It is advantageous to me to have as many employees directly delivering services to patients as possible. I would prefer to have 80 employees and 6 administrative staff, as opposed to 10.

I Set Out to Tie Creative Compensation to These Metrics, such as Rewarding Positive Patient Outcomes.

Metrics inform every aspect of my organization, including my marketing. They help me to clearly define where patients began and what shape their journey took. If you can take your metrics and layer over them a compelling story that helps illustrate the story behind the metrics, you will have something truly magical.

Another important consideration is *patient referral statistics.* One of my clients was recently reviewing their online presence and noticed a considerable drop in their search engine rankings over the past six months. My client had outsourced their search engine optimization services to a third-party company, which had evidently grown complacent over time.

The company had been working with this vendor for nearly 12 years. I asked if they had seen the metrics. The client responded with a dumbfounded, "No."

When I reviewed the numbers myself, I said, "You just had the worst 6 months in the last 12 years."

What were they doing to address it? They didn't have the first idea of how to proceed—and neither did the experts they had hired. It goes to illustrate how you have to hold not just yourself and your team accountable, but your partners as well. After all, nobody else is going to have as much ever invested—personally or financially—in your venture as you.

This goes to underscore the need for you to go under the hood and really understand the nitty gritty of your business, even seemingly arcane areas that you may have little background or interest in. Get familiar with all of the financial statistics—your profit and loss, your expenses, and your cash flow. All of these are critical for you to have under control.

Key Financial Metrics

Let's talk about some key financial metrics.

There's your *balance sheet,* which provides a comprehensive picture of the financial condition of your organization. On the last day of a given accounting period, you generally use the balance sheet to evaluate if your total liabilities and equity equals your assets. This exercise will help you to uncover your debt, outstanding amounts owed, your cash on hand, and other crucial metrics of financial health.

Income statement – I live and die by this one. This tool provides clear information about the financial results of operations during a given reporting period, such as your profit, loss, and revenue.

It informs the reader of items such as:

- Revenue produced from various sources

- The costs to produce the good or services

- Overhead expenses

- Profit or loss for the period of time

Net income is another important consideration, giving you a clear understanding of everything that remains after all of your expenses are paid out.

Seven Statistics for Survival, Success, and Scalability

1. Cash Flow Analysis

2. Profit and Loss – The Meat on the Bone Margin

3. The Patient Aging Report

4. Marketing/Referral Effectiveness

5. Payer Mix

6. Productivity

7. Cancellation Report

1. Cash Flow Analysis

A challenging aspect of running a profit and loss statement in a healthcare environment is that you often are doing it on a quarterly or biannual or even on annual basis. It will be very important to gain a thorough understanding of cash flow through a cash flow analysis.

Let me give you an example. Let's say you are running a healthcare practice. You bill a thousand units for the month to insurance providers. Of those 1,000 units, you may get paid 50 percent of your fees in 30 days, but as for the remaining 50 percent, you may get paid over the next 180 days. In addition, there may be claims that get denied and paid. That reality can make it tough to provide an accurate analysis of the profit and loss for that particular month. It can sometimes take as long as six months or a year to really determine what the financial picture looks like.

This reality underscores how important cash flow is to our industry. It allows you to gauge if more money is coming in than going out. Your revenue might be coming in for January from production that you did three months ago.

What you often find when people are launching practices is that their cash flow is really awful for the first 90 days if they're taking payer sources that pay delayed. That's why I stress my metric that 60 percent of your revenue must be collected in 30 days or less. Run with that model and you will be effective.

So, ultimately when we're looking at the cash flow, we want to know how much cash was the result of the sales, how much was spent, how much money was borrowed, and how much was invested.

In my history in business, we have never missed a payroll, and I'm very proud to say that. All of our employees get paid every other Friday, and they all get paid.

2. Profit and Loss – The Meat on the Bone Margin

I call this the meat on the bone, margin—how much meat on that bone? So, if you're getting a 100 percent markup and you want to wait a little longer, that's one thing. But if you're getting a one percent margin, you better collect that in 30 days 100 percent. What's the meat on your business's bone?

3. The Patient Aging Report

How much money is owed? Is it 30 days outstanding, 60 days, 90 days to you? What is your aging report?

4. Marketing/Referral Effectiveness

You can spend a lot of money in marketing these days. If you have no way to measure how it's working with clear metrics, you need to make that an immediate priority. This is how you formulate the return on investment analysis as it relates to your marketing efforts. I recently worked with a marketing expert that shared he guarantees 10 new patients per month for $10,000, but the problem is the business he was pitching would not even make $1,000 on the lifetime of a patient. So this marketing action would have been a loss. If the lifetime value of a patient is worth $750 and the acquisition cost of the client was $1,000, then clearly this was not the right marketing strategy.

5. Payer Mix

Run your payer mix—how does it break down? What's your diversification of payer mix? How reliant are you on one type of payer? I used to have 54 percent Blue Cross as my funding source. I recognized that I needed to diversify where my revenue was coming from; otherwise, I was going to live or die on that relationship.

6. Productivity

Of course, it is essential to closely track your productivity with clear metrics and data related to the return on investment for your time and resources in your priority areas.

7. Cancellation Report

Evaluating cancellations and how to overcome the cancellations is so important. I believe that as a baseline, cancellations should generally stay under 3-5 percent as a rule of thumb depending on your business model and profitability percentages.

Metrics and Creative Compensation

I pride myself on creating competitive compensation packages that include exchange in abundance through creative compensations strategies ranging from benefits, productivity incentives, learning opportunities, and employee culture.

But I recognize I need to go above and beyond at times. That's why I put in incentives for performance as well.

That can include exploring mechanisms like profit sharing and productivity incentives. I have made it a priority to create buy-in, empower flexibility, incentivize clinical growth, and motivate word-of-mouth referrals, knowing how all important that first impression is that you receive from a team member's recommendation of their employer.

Money speaks to all of us but so do intangibles like purpose, learning, growth, and making a difference in this world. Being able to tie rewards to your metrics is a recipe for success as long as it builds on the culture of your company.

Top Tools for Tracking Private Practice Metrics

Keep in mind some handy tools that I like and personally use for tracking private practice metrics.

- Electronic Medical Record / Practice Management Platforms

- Spreadsheet Software, such as Microsoft Excel (Data Dump with Pivot Tables, etc.)

- Outcome Tracking Platform (i.e. FOTO)

- Key Performance Indicator Platform (i.e. KPI Fire)

All are great resources and well worth considering for your practice.

CHAPTER 7

Developing Your Optimum Payer Mix and Building Your Billing Department

"Rule number 1: Never lose money.
Rule number 2: Never forget rule number 1."
—Warren Buffet

Now that we've nailed down your metrics, it's time to build your payer mix.

Let's begin by considering what type of payer sources you may be looking at.

The most common examples that healthcare private practices look at are commercial health insurance payers. These include players like Blue Cross, United-Healthcare, Health Net, and so on.

We also have to consider government sources such as Medicare and Medicaid.

In addition, there are all the nuances to consider in the other options—workers' compensation insurance, personal injury, government contracts, staffing contracts, grant funding (if you're in the non-profit space), and so on. Please keep in mind that other service-based private practices have both public and private funding sources ranging from state funding, federal grants, city grants, private pay, and more.

The reason we want to diversify your payer mix is simple—you don't want to put all your apples in one basket. Each of the different payers have different pros and cons; the key is to diversify your income based on cash flow, margin, and client retention.

I have said it before and I will say it again. The key principle to developing your optimum payer mix is that you want 60 percent of the payer mix paying you 100 percent within 30 days or less. This is simply crucial.

To be clear, when I say 30 days or less, that is 30 days from the date of service. As you build your billing department, it is very important to get those claims in on-time, right away.

One of the questions that I often hear is, "Brandon how do I get these commercial contracts? I'm interested in playing in the insurance game—where do I begin?"

There are no shortage of factors to consider—your National Provider Identifier, your tax ID, and your Medicare number to name but a few.

It helps to begin by first clearly identifying what contracts you are interested in. Do you want Blue Cross? Do you want Blue Shield? Depending on your state, there may just be one governing body to work with.

What are the other contacts that you're interested in? Are they small? Are they big? Are they national? Are they state level? Do you need a grant writer to submit for certain funding sources? Are you contracting with a private entity such as a preschool or an assisted living facility? These are all things that you want to look at. You then want to identify the contracting body.

Something that you might not realize is that certain insurances, depending on where you're located, would work directly with you as you assume the role of a contractor. Certain other players work through alternative payer sources, such as Optum-Health, which typically is the governing body for United-Healthcare.

When I was first starting out in California, our initial contract with Blue Cross actually required us to go through a network called PTPN. There are many networks that you want to research. One thing that you should keep in mind is identifying your credential and needs. There are several credentialing requirements when you're partnering with these contracting bodies, whether it be CAQH credentialing or direct credentialing with the insurance company. Start to look at those options and do your research.

You will also want to get up to speed on the process of submitting a formal or informal RFP—Request for Proposal. It is absolutely crucial that you target what that payer source is looking for and what your niche is. Clearly explain how you deliver medical necessity, what your clinical outcomes are, and what separates you from the competition. As an example, I might stress that I bring together a team of bilingual clinicians in a multidisciplinary outpatient clinic and that I bring a strong track record.

Another key consideration is to ensure that your billing department is on top of its game—whether it's in-house or third-party, you have to be ready and able to show that you're prepared. The other consideration to keep in mind is that your documentation policies are together. Do you have clinical documentation set forth that's going to align with what that funding source is looking for? It's important that you identify the goals of your clients in terms of how they relate to the payer source.

Medical Necessity

This is a very important factor if you are playing in the health insurance game. It's essential that all your goals are targeting the medical necessity of the patient—whether you're an occupational therapist targeting functional goals, or if you're a mental health professional working on mental health goals related to the medical necessity and the mental health of the client. In any of these instances, all of these supporting details are essential in your documentation. Remember—your documentation and your clinical outcomes are how you justify them paying for your services.

The next question that I often hear is this—how do I negotiate with payer sources? I was recently on the phone with a private practice in Houston. The owner has been in business for 18 years, but she still came to me with questions from time to time. She asked me, "How do I negotiate with these commercial payer sources?"

I replied, "Have you ever asked for an increase to your reimbursement rate?"

She said that in 18 years she had never had an increase and had never requested one.

I then reiterated to make sure that I was hearing her correctly and said, "Seriously, you have never had an increase to your reimbursement rate?"

She replied, "No, they've only taken money away from me." I also confirmed that she had never even asked for a rate increase.

I followed up by saying, "Well, if you don't ask, they assume that you're satisfied with your rate."

There are several keys to negotiating with payer sources. The first consideration to keep in mind is you have to show the data: you need strong outcome metrics and strong key performance indicators.

You can't just make claims—you also need to have qualitative and quantitative analysis to back up why they need you, how you're going to provide them a strong return on investment in your proposal, that you have clinical bios supporting the integrity of your team, the background of your team, how you differentiate yourself, and samples of your documentation. I say all of that because that's ultimately what's going to justify that you're doing quality work.

I always say your payer sources are focused on money as well as satisfying the necessities of their clientele. That's why you need to make a clear call to action. They don't care that your expenses are going up or that your clinicians want more money. They care that you can deliver a more effective product than anyone else and ultimately save them money if they pay you appropriately.

Here's an example: "Hey Blue Cross—I'll tell you what. If I can get $25 more per visit, I can deliver a full 60-minute visit where I'm going to actually increase the clinical outcomes, so that I can discharge your clients sooner. Rather than you paying for 18 visits, I'll get it done in 12—so that over the long run, you're going to save money and have clients happier." The math works out like this: 18 visits at $75 per visit costs Blue Cross a total of $1,350, but $100 per visit for 12 visits only costs them $1200. You can tell me that they are only saving $150, but they are also getting their clients to optimum outcomes faster. That is the secret recipe in playing to their pain points.

That is how you negotiate a payer source to align with their goals. If you provide them metrics and detail a finite period of time that you're going to accomplish their needs, it's a win-win for all.

You win because you actually are growing your margin where you can deliver a higher quality service. *The client* wins because they're getting better services and their financial investment gets stronger. So clearly it is important to think about each party and what they're trying to accomplish as you attack any negotiation.

At the end of the day, the payer source has the power. It's like I always say—no money, no honey. The payer has the power, so you have to understand what their driving forces are. You have to understand what they're looking for—generally it is fundamentally about saving money while still meeting clinical guidelines. Therefore, you have to really make a claim that what you're exchanging with them is in abundance and important.

The Secret to Creating a Cash Positive Business Model

All of these are crucial steps in helping you to maintain a steady, reliable flow of cash that allows you to meet payroll without concern and keep the lights on.

- Identify Your Niche

- Offer Value Added Programs

- Diversify Your Cash Flow

- Build A Program with "Mail Box Money" Opportunities (Gym Memberships)

- Create, Execute, & Empower The Customer Experience

- Make Your Metrics Matter

- Manage Your Market Retention

- Continue To Innovate

Pay special attention to the need to carefully define your niche. For example, I have a feeding practice that specializes in working with infants that have swallowing disorders. That is a clear and powerful value proposition for parents struggling with this issue. Our niche and focus on this topic set us apart from all of the generalists vying with us in the market.

What are the value added programs that you're offering? How do you exchange value to a client that they can't get through their current health insurance offerings? What are programs that you're going to deliver?

By diversifying your cash flow, you can build a program that generates significant mailbox money—that is to say, revenue that's coming in that doesn't take manpower. This type of passive income is the most powerful means available to generating real wealth. You only have so many hours in the day and so much energy—if you can figure out to how to keep generating revenue as you sleep, you are in prime position to succeed. An example would be creating home exercise videos or apps that you can spend upfront time developing, and then you can kick back while they continue to generate cash for you.

I want you to create, execute, and empower a great customer experience. One of the components that I often find really valuable in the customer experience is preventative health. Focus not only on rehabilitating your patients, but also on putting resources together to prevent future challenges that they may face. Look not just at them, but at all of their surroundings. Maybe you're incorporating some diet strategies, or maybe you're incorporating some fitness. There are so many different ways that you can embrace preventative health in today's environment. Let's manage your market retention. I urge you to evaluate how long people are staying within your program and how you foster transitional care that supports them in a long run of their life.

Finally, keep in mind that last secret to a cash positive business model—innovation. How do we think outside the box? How do we offer something that is fundamentally different from everything else being offered on the marketplace? How do we relate with not just this next generation of millennials but other generations? Innovation is key.

Building Your Billing Department

Whether you outsource your billing department or you keep these services in-house, you need to identify what your needs are.

The decision to outsource these functions is generally dependent on such factors as:

- Scalability

- Complexity of Payer Mix

- Fixed Overhead Vs. Variable Overhead

- Liability & Control

- Ability to Manage and Ensure Accountability

When you're outsourcing your billing duties, keep in mind that they will generally become variable costs—you will pay a cost that ranges anywhere from 6 to 12 percent of all the income you collect.

With that in mind, I recommend that many smaller firms work with an external partner—as long as they have strong measures in place to hold that third-party company accountable.

Another important factor to consider, of course, is liability and control. If you give the keys to your billing department away, make sure that you do maintain some mechanisms to keep control and accountability.

It is very important to keep in mind how a billing department is organized.

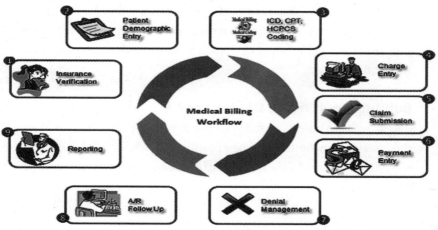

A few of the takeaways here include remembering to make sure you always verify the insurance benefits before you bring a partner on.

As for who actually enters the chargers, this will typically be performed by an in-house staffer. Your front desk person will actually enter the charges based on the way that the clinician delivers the service or the clinician may even enter it. Upon submission of the claim, third party actors usually get involved in double-checking the charge entry and troubleshooting any problems that emerge.

They can play a key role in reevaluating outstanding payments, challenges, and common mistakes.

Something to keep in mind about your billing department is that you're painting a realistic expectation for your clients of their risk. That risk doesn't fall on the provider—it falls on the client. That's something critical to clarify from the outset.

I always say that I maintain this rule of thumb in life: it's called under promise, over deliver. Paint the expectation for what insurance won't cover; make it clear that if within 60 days a bill doesn't get paid, the client will be held responsible. As you look at all of the pieces here, you want to make sure that your method of holding the client accountable aligns with your insurance contracts. This is very important.

I always say when you're negotiating an insurance contract, make sure that you're truly negotiating; after all, an insurance contract is always written on behalf of the insurance company. Therefore, you sometimes need a third-party person to look at those contracts to give you feedback, to understand how to negotiate that contract to your favor, and identify all of the resources out there that can help you with that.

At Wellness Works Management Partners, we have a team of people that supports clinics just like you in making sure that you're signing quality contracts.

Top Five Mistakes of Private Practice Owners in Billing

Some mistakes are inevitable in life and business, but it's far preferable to learn from others' mistakes rather than making your own. Here are a few common pitfalls I see among private practice owners when it comes to billing in particular.

#1 - The private practice owner gives away the keys to the castle.

I see it all the time, and I'm sure you've seen it. They literally say something to the effect of, "I don't know billing. Here are my keys. You go ahead and do it. Just get me paid, please."

Don't do this. I beg you! Ultimately I've never seen a practice give away the keys to the castle and not go on to have major issues in this department. Even though you may outsource things, I want you to hold your partners fully accountable. I want you to measure your reports and your metrics. Always be aware of what's outstanding and what must get paid. Hold them accountable.

#2 - A lack of organization leads to claims not getting submitted on time.

I see *this* one all the time as well. I walk into a billing department. The first thing I do is actually ask the owner, "Can I look in the drawers of your billing department?"

When they ask why, I reply, "Because I'm going to know how chaotic that department is based on the organization of those drawers."

They reply to me, "Be our guest."

This is usually when I walk in and take out a stack of papers. What I find is months and months and months of claims that people have just essentially brushed to the side. They keep telling themselves, I'm going to get to them, I'm going to get to them, and I'm going to get to them.

No, they aren't. They need organization to their claims department. That is very important across the board—in infrastructure, systems, accountability. Absolutely nothing should be in drawers. I repeat, nothing should be in your drawers.

#3 - Lack of transparency and outstanding balances for patients increasing significantly resulting in horrific public relations and financial challenges for the patient.

The next challenge is a lack of transparency. I have plenty of experience with this including a previous practice that I was a part of. I remember coming in one day. I called up our third-party billing company, and asked, "What's our longest outstanding claim?"

The answer was, "Huh? What do you mean? I repeated myself, and the owner of the billing company said, "Brandon we have bills that are well over a year."

I couldn't believe my ears. I said, "What? Where are the bills?" Do the patients know about this?

The billing company shared that they had not contacted the patients because they were still working with the insurance companies to try and resolve the issue and felt confident it would get resolved. I was fuming because transparency is the key; how do you go to a patient years later sharing that they have an outstanding bill that could not be collected from the insurance company and ask for them to pay up? You end up writing off claims that are that old. Also, please keep in mind that a third-party billing company typically only chases the "lowest-hanging fruit" because after all they only make money based on what they collect.

I found out that one of the client's balance was over $2,500 and the claims were over a year old. It might not seem like so much in the grand scheme of things for a large and growing practice, but trying to collect that level of money is nearly impossible and can break your bottom line in a low margin game. I always say that you need to have your transparency in place both within your team, your vendors, and your clients. Cut to today; I never let an accounts receivable exceed $500 per client without a sign off from the client—never. You should strive for the same policy. This was a nightmare experience that I still wake up to from time to time. I have learned from that experience and would never allow for that to occur again, whether it is for my own practice or one of my clients.

#4 - Private practice puts production as priority and signs a bad contract.

The next issue that I often see is that a private practice puts production as the priority and signs a bad contract. A client of mine in Houston exemplified this problem. They would sign contracts that were absolutely awful.

When I asked them why, they replied, "Because we needed the patient volume. Brandon, you don't understand."

"I understand that you basically just paid for those clients to get services, because you lost money on every visit. I can bring 300 new clients a day for you if you want to give your services for free—even more."

You want to take Medicaid? In some places you can get lots and lots of clients just rolling down your doorstep. The problem is that you're not going to get paid in many cases for sometimes six months, nine months, a year...or even at all depending on location and the contract. Don't sign a bad contract.

The easy route is to say, "I'm taking a contract that's just a wealth of leads." However, that might not be the best long-term strategy. I find that ROI is more important than playing the numbers game in today's healthcare environment. In our next section of the book, as we delve more into marketing, we will talk about how to build your client base. I would rather you invest in marketing than invest in bad contracts that funnel your clients.

#5 - Confusion, confusion, and more confusion

The final mistake that I see so frequently made is a refusal to resolve or at least diffuse confusion. I see it all the time. Confusion can have a truly outsized impact on the condition of your private practice. A great example of this is billed charges versus contracted charges. For those of you who are playing in the insurance game, you understand that you create a fee schedule based on billed charges, because there are some insurances that just pay you a percentage of those billed charges.

But your billed charges don't necessarily equal what you are expecting to get paid. Sometimes I inflate my payer expense and my pay list because I want to get 80 percent of the highest rate—for example, I'm charging $225, but then you have contracted rates at $75. Remember, don't evaluate your billed charges—evaluate your contracted rates and what you actually anticipate getting paid.

Strategies for Billing Success

Now that you are more familiar with the common mistakes, what are some ways that you can avoid them and set yourself up for success?

One way is to ensure that your private practice owner reviews key billing metrics weekly, inclusive of what's going on in your aging report. What are the claims submitted for the prior week? How much money is coming in? Are there any outpoints? If you see anything that is not traditional—anything that you see that needs to get taken care of—jump on it sooner than later. You won't regret addressing it quickly and as soon as possible.

The next effective strategy for the private practice owner is to institute a program for transparency with patient's outstanding balance, including a cap. Remember that a good best practice is to set that cap at $500, which you should make clear on the first visit. Make sure that clients understand that the risk is on them.

You can also set yourself up to success by utilizing cash flow metrics. You can incentivize both your patients and employees for the outcomes you seek through creating buy-in and leveraging creative compensation for your employees.

When it comes to the payer mix, maybe you can actually

incentivize your customers. You can essentially say, "Hey! I'm going to offer a discount. Buy 20 coaching sessions with me, and I'll give you a discount." Collect the money upfront—you have instant positive cash flow.

The last consideration to think about is to consider an electronic medical record system. As more of the economy is increasingly digitized, this will only grow in importance. An electronic medical record system is a key to not only your metrics, but to electronic submission, claims submission, and real-time claim info. You can set yourself apart from competitors by implementing a robust patient portal in which patients can access their charts. Take steps now to be an early adopter and you can reap great rewards in the future.

CHAPTER 8

———◆>✕<◆———

Maximizing Your Marketing, Scale to the Finish Line

"An organization's ability to learn, and translate that learning into action rapidly, is the ultimate competitive advantage."
—Jack Welch, *Former CEO, General Electric*

At this point, we've built your foundation and have looked at your metrics. We've talked about your payer mix and your vision is becoming rapidly clearer. Now it is time that we look in greater depth at marketing.

This might not seem like the most important item with everything else that falls into your purview as a leader. You might assume that good work will speak for itself and word will get out. But today in an era of hyper competition on the internet, it is more crucial than ever that you can articulately tell a compelling story about the value proposition of your business. It is more often than not the business that can tell the most compelling story will ultimately win.

Again, look at the resurgence of Apple in the 1990s. The

company had struggled for years; as odd as it is to consider from today's vantage point, Microsoft was considered the far more innovative competitor at the time. The fortunes only began to turn with the return of founder Steve Jobs. Jobs' genius wasn't as much in technological knowledge, as much as it was telling an effective and compelling story about how Apple products could foster creativity. Jobs' presentations were unlike anything else seen in the typically staid arena of corporate presentations—they were like rock concerts in themselves. They turned consumers into true evangelists for the brand, a testament to the power of marketing and savvy PR.

So let's start out by briefly defining marketing. That might not sound necessary as you likely have a strong idea in your head of what the word means, but there are so many miscommunications and misunderstandings of what marketing truly represents. I want to give you a clear definition to ensure that you and I are speaking the same language.

Ergo, we will define marketing as the activity, set of institutions, and processes for creating, communicating, delivering, and exchanging offerings that have value for customers, clients, partners and society at large.

Under the umbrella of this marketing, there are two areas that we often look at in particular.

One is *public relations*, which refers to that form of communication management that seeks to make use of publicity and other non-paid forms of promotion and information to influence feelings, opinions, and beliefs about a company.

The other key area is *advertising*, which we'll characterize as the placement of an announcement or a message by business firms, non-profit organizations, government agencies, and individuals who seek to persuade an audience to consider their products or services.

A key distinction to keep in mind is that in public relations, the goal is generally to get someone talking about you. An example might be working with a journalist to encourage them to write a profile detailing how amazing your practice is. Advertising, on the other hand, is the art of speaking directly to someone, such as through buying an ad in the same magazine, or purchasing ad space on a billboard.

Whatever the medium or platform, this area fundamentally all comes down to communication. That's what marketing is about. It's a form of communication. Your brand is a communication. The marketing material is a communication. Your brochures, your flyers, your websites, and your public relations, it's all about communication. Advertisements can include blogs, newsletters, thank you cards, welcome cards, marketing gift baskets—all of it falls under the rubric of communication.

When you go to that special event and you get that swag bag, even that is a form of communication. So think of marketing as a form of communication. As you create your strategy, what do you want to communicate? Think to the big picture, not just short-term tactical wins. What's the response that you want from the communication and how do you measure the effectiveness of the communication?

I often refer to a word called "Publics." Just to ensure that we are all talking the same language, these are communities of people at large, organized as a group that have a direct or indirect association with an organization. Customers are a public, your employees are a public, your investors are a public, the media can be a public, students are a public, and then there are publics within publics.

We could say on a governing level that students are a public. To break this down further, one could say student physicians are a public or pediatric occupational therapist students are a public. There are simply so many different ways to breakdown that public.

In terms of private practice and defining your marketing publics, I want you to think of the following categories:

- External Referral Partners (Broken down further by category such as doctors, psychologists, fitness instructors, teachers, etc.)

- Internal Customers (Clients currently receiving your services.)

- Advertising Channels (Schools, gyms, media, etc.)

- Employees

All of these can be broken down further. For example, we've got advertising channels as a public—these could include that sign outside of a school where you show that you're a sponsor. It might be in a magazine like a parent or a fitness magazine or something that's related to your public that you're trying to communicate to. Again, there are so many different marketing publics. You will want to start to define them and build your list as you create your market strategy.

As we look back on the history of marketing, an awful lot has changed over the years. I think that it's so important that we do a quick glance back so that you understand where we've come from and where we're going in terms of how we utilize marketing to our benefit.

Until fairly recently marketing actually consisted mostly of outbound marketing, essentially talking *at* a customer without giving them much of an outlet for communicating in return. This was the key trend line of the period right up until around the 1990s, when the internet boom really took off and exciting new outlets emerged for digital marketing.

Prior to 1900, everything was defined by printed advertising. We had magazines emerging in 1730s. In 1830s we had posters beginning to emerge—1867 is the earliest recording of an actual billboard rental. Then in 1922 we started to get quite a bit of a change when radio advertising came in.

Just imagine in 1922, hearing your first radio advertisement. It might have been for Sears or a car dealership. Whatever the first ad was, it likely seared itself into your memory.

1941 saw the first wave of television advertising, further cementing cutting-edge (for the time) marketing concepts into the psyche of the viewer.

Although we have continued to advance in our technology over the years, the essential value proposition remains the same—creating a need for a product or service in the mind of the potential customer. That fundamental goal of connecting with the customer was very much present even then.

Television advertising increased in scope and sophistication over the 1950s into the '70s, as portrayed so memorably on the hit AMC series *Mad Men*. Then in 1970, something came about that to this day still drives us all crazy.

Do you know what I'm talking about yet? That's right—telemarketing. All of us hate getting that call. You can't tell me that you don't! Even though they think they're talking to us, they're talking *at* us.

How many of you have gotten that call asking, "What are you planning to do with your house today? Well, I've got a construction person in your neighborhood who can help you update your home." Are they really talking to us? Not really. They're indeed talking *at* us. That's why telemarketing has been dying out over recent decades. We fortunately have expanded legal protections that remove many of us from call lists and most of us have the ability to screen our calls to avoid unwanted sales pitches.

As we progress through time in 1981 to 1984, IBM introduced the first personal computer. In 1984, we saw a revolutionary ad that came out during the Super Bowl for Apple, formally launching the era of the blockbuster television ad during major sporting events. Apple revolutionized their market by creating a great customer experience and addressing them through unconventional marketing that broke the tired old constraints of the genre.

In 1990, we started to see mobile networks growing in importance. All of a sudden around the window of 1995-1997, search marketing formally launched. In 1998, Google introduced its first platform of ranking pages for search engine optimization—how much would we all give to return back to that early period and make a big investment in the company's growth!

In 2000, the true game changer happened. After years of doomsday warnings from market watchers concerned at sky-high valuation on companies of dubious value (think of the now infamous pets.com), the dot com bubble finally burst. All of a sudden after 2000, outbound marketing transitioned to become inbound marketing. More of us began to utilize the Internet in a whole new way, entering a brave new era of information sharing.

User-centered design and collaboration became the new rules of the road. Suddenly effective marketing was not about throwing something in our face; instead it was about us communicating, talking, and sharing our stories. The very idea of word-of-mouth marketing took a whole new form because referrals became a communication of inbound marketing through technology. In 2003, email users won the anti-spammer rights, which obviously changed things profoundly. Yes, you and I both know that we still receive a million emails a day, so clearly there is much more progress that must be made.

It is easy to forget sometimes just how dramatically the entire economic landscape has shifted in a comparatively short amount of time. It was only around 2003 to 2004 that social media began to truly launch in earnest. In 2005, Google branded its analytics. In 2006, Hub Spot launched, along with Twitter. That same year, Amazon sales topped $10 billion, and in 2007, 295 million subscribers signed onto mobile 3G networks. We were now not merely online—the very nature of how we communicated and processed information about the world had been completely revolutionized.

For those who don't know, advertising has reached an all-time high for digital media. The market has reached a point where we can track exactly what people are interested in and what they're looking for. We can now create conversations with them with a snap of a finger—pretty incredible when you consider how far we have come from the days of radio. As we approached the years 2010 and 2012, we all know that social media engagement has been growing. As of 2014 and beyond, suddenly 67 percent of people check their phone without a notification even pinging them to do so. Marketing has expanded and the opportunities are endless to create change in our community through reaching new publics.

This leads us to consider the very role of digital media in the 21st century. You should keep in mind that digital media has taken over as one of the leading marketing platforms in today's private practice environment. Our industry has been just as touched by these developments as every other sector of the economy. The reasons for this include cost, market penetration, and flexibility.

You can also ensure much greater accountability because of the built-in metrics that inform you of every granular detail on how your strategy is unfolding; for example, you can find out that you have had 1,200 clicks in six minutes for a particular ad or track the conversion rate bringing someone from an ad to your website.

We must also never lose sight of the unique role of technology in the human condition. Go to a restaurant today—sit and count how many people look at their phone while they're eating. Sometimes it can look as though everyone is bowing their heads in prayer to our new Digital Gods. Whether you like it or not, technology has profoundly revolutionized the human condition. We know that it is clearly influencing the way that we grow and the human condition as a whole. As we see in the digital marketing realm in particular, we can do so much at the snap of a finger that we could have never imagined before.

Examples of Digital Marketing in Action

There is a wide range of tools and outlets that you can explore leveraging for your business, many that you are likely familiar with from your own personal usage. These include:

- Facebook

- Google

- Yelp

- Blogging

- Pinterest

- YouTube

- Twitter

- Content Marketing Search Engine Optimization (SEO)

- Search Engine Marketing (SEM)

- Affiliate Marketing

- Email Marketing

It can be overwhelming to consider which tools and platforms are most effective for spreading your particular message. This is where the work that you have already invested upfront in conducting a thorough market analysis will be so crucial for your future success. Refer back to the plans you laid out in your business plan. Referring to your planning in this stage should enable you to create a marketing budget and plan that reflects your broader strategic goals for your practice.

I urge you to play for the long-term here. Don't just look for the quick fix. Don't just make a cavalier decision to drop $1,000 today and "see how it goes." Marketing takes time. You must maintain a marathon mentality as in any other aspect of your business. Recognize that your budget will often represent an aspirational statement—as opportunities and challenges emerge, everything has a way of ending up costing more. It all starts with a quarter and ends with a $100 bill. It's just the way it is; the really important consideration to remember when you're creating your marketing budget is that you know what your return on investment is for your product or service that you offer.

If I have to spend $1,000 to make $1 per visit, I don't know if it's worthwhile. But if you ask me to drop $1,000 and I have a 50 percent margin, we're talking a whole new ball game. Understanding your margin in your service delivery will allow you to help establish your marketing budget.

The last point I urge you to consider is creating a marketing action list categorized by your marketing public. Anticipate when you're going to complete the percentage of your budget that you're allocating and a projected return on investment. I believe in digital marketing, but I also believe in guerrilla marketing. I met with just about every pediatrician in a 60-mile radius of Los Angeles when I had my clinic. Invest in some shoe leather and get out there—meet, have lunch, buy lunch, bring those nurses your pens, bring them your pads or paper, make those relationships. It's not about quantity; it's about quality and consistency in marketing—as well as the ability to measure the effectiveness and pivot when needed.

A common mistake that private practice owners make is that they essentially put the cart before the horse. They invest then find themselves all alone. They drop as much as $10,000-$15,000 into branding and marketing and websites and everything… yet they have no organization, no structure. They create a bad client experience that leads to bad word of mouth, and it takes years to dig out of that hole. Remember the old adage: Measure twice, cut once.

Go back through your strategic plan carefully before you spend a dime on marketing. Make sure you have your t's crossed and your i's dotted. Private practice owners waste their marketing budget by treating their business like a marathon. Just because someone promised you 100 leads tomorrow, it doesn't mean that it's a good idea. What are the conversion rates of those leads? What's the value and can you handle the business?

I once took a contract that tripled my business, but I wasn't ready for it and ultimately it cost me far more in cleaning up systems. So as we say, slow and steady wins the race. Be very cautious of supply and demand business growth decisions.

This is something that many healthcare professionals tell me: "Brandon, I'm moving here because there's no other provider in the area."

This is often a mistake. For one thing, they often have not done their due diligence to truly determine that there is no other provider in the area. I always say that if something looks too good to be true it probably is.

Another important consideration is understanding that just because there's a demand doesn't mean that there's the market value there. Take the time to truly understand the return on investment you can expect given current amounts of supply and demand.

Scaling to numbers can be very costly. Sometimes that 10 x 10 office that you're running for 12 months by yourself is more financially viable than that practice with 25 employees and spending so much money to scale and support that market demand. My advice is to resist signing up for a bad funding contract based on the supply and demand opportunities. Instead, pick a business location based on a wide viewpoint, not a narrow perspective of supply and demand. Simply determining that there is not another provider in a 50-mile radius is not enough.

Don't make the big vision investment, because everyone else is doing it. I hear it all the time. "Brandon, I saw your company advertise at this trade show, so I figured I should do it." I am in a different point in my business model than you are—just as my business might not be in the same business model as other consultants. We're all playing a different game to a certain extent, or we're a different place in the game. Follow the path that is right for you.

Don't make marketing decisions based on playing the numbers game. Just because you can add a thousand new visits next month doesn't mean that it's viable. Run the numbers, run the metrics. Measure twice, cut once.

Big Picture Marketing Strategies

Your Brand:

- Know It

- Embody It

- Ensure There Is Continuity

- Communicate It

Create Your Communication Channels:

- Engage The Dialogue (Don't Talk "At" But "To")

- Know Your Publics

- Timeliness Of Communication Matters

- Acknowledgement Of Communication

Create a Memorable Experience:

- Experience Is The Secret To Referrals

- Results Is Part Of The Experience

- Surveys and Metrics Are How Your Evaluate Your Experience

Walk Before You Run:

- Pick Your Marketing Mediums Wisely Based On Research, Anticipated ROI, Experience

- Consistency in Marketing Is Essential To Evaluate Results Appropriately

- Know Your End Product Goal Precisely When Launching Marketing Campaigns

- Don't Put All Your Eggs in The Same Basket

- Don't Get Complacent with Your Marketing

Relationships – The Million Dollar Marketing Recipe:

- Relationships Is Truly The Key To Long Term Results

- Nurture And Invest In Your Relationships

- Acknowledgements Go A Long Way In Our Business!

Leverage a variety of tools to communicate your brand. Remember that timeliness of communication matters; when a client emails you that they're interested, don't wait a week to get back to them. I like to respond in 48 hours or less if I can. I at least provide an acknowledgement: "I've received your communication, and I'll get back to you in the next week." But if you wait a week, they're already calling five other people.

The next thing I want you to think about is how to create a memorable experience. We've talked about this with Apple—experience is the secret to referrals. Every part of the experience for your customers, from the moment they walk through the door, will influence the impressions they are left with.

The world of marketing is fundamentally built on two things: *surveys and metrics*. Leveraging these tools will let you know if something is working or if you need to pivot.

There is a lot to take on when launching your own practice. You should strive to walk before you run. Pick your marketing mediums wisely and base them on research. Understand the ROI on the experience—consistency in marketing pays off. Know your end product goal and how many clients you're trying to attract with that marketing action.

Don't put all your eggs in one basket. Diversify your marketing actions and stay consistent.

Don't get complacent with your marketing. The other day I was with a client who has been implementing the same marketing strategy for eight years. I asked her, "Is it effective?"

She replied, "I don't know, but I'm afraid to stop." That's scary to me. She is spending $3,000 a month on marketing, and she *thinks* it's working. You have to *know* it is working.

Relationships make up a million dollar marketing recipe. I would rather you invest $10,000 in solid relationships that will pay it forward than $10,000 in just talking at people. Invest in the relationships. It's been the key to my success; it'll be the key to your success. Nurture and invest in all of those people.

Acknowledgment goes a long way with people. All of my strategic relationships and clients hold a very special place in my heart. When you work with me, you truly are part of my family. I take care of you like I'm taking care of a family member. After all, I started in the healthcare space because of my family.

Now everyone I work with is part of my family. You should be treating your publics the same way. Find your customers and treat them like gold.

CHAPTER 9

Secrets to Recruitment, Hiring, and - Of Course - The Management of People

"People ask the difference between a leader and a boss.
The leader leads, and the boss drives."
—Teddy Roosevelt

The most important decisions that you will ever make involve hiring. There is only so much that you can accomplish as a single individual. In order to truly achieve greatness, it requires building a team that works as one in executing against a single defined goal.

There's a famous story from NASA in the 1960s that I think about often. President Kennedy was visiting the headquarters to get a sense of how the mission he had set to land a lunar module was unfolding. At one point, he broke away from the assembled dignitaries and carefully orchestrated public relations to greet a custodian mopping the floor. The President extended his hand and said, "I'm John Kennedy. What have you been doing at NASA?"

The janitor shook his hand and replied, "Mr. President, I'm

helping to put a man on the moon."

When you can convey a clear sense of the mission to be achieved and communicate to each member of your team why their contributions matter, you will have created something truly extraordinary.

At the end of the day, we are in the people business. It's all about people. Everything you do is about people, whether you're a healthcare practitioner, a chiropractor, an occupational therapist, physical therapist, speech therapist, nutritionist—you name it. Even with all of your advanced health or technological expertise, you are all about people.

So when we recruit, when we hire, when we manage—don't forget that. We're not just picking up a pencil from Staples. We're hiring a person and that person is going to represent you, your brand, and the practice. They will ultimately be responsible in some way or another in relationship to the customer experience.

One of my famous metaphors is that recruiting and hiring is like the bread of a sandwich, but the management of people? That's peanut butter and jelly. So, it's very important that you understand that hiring the right people is obviously really important, but how you manage them is everything. No one likes stale bread, so make your bread choices really smart. If you don't put the right jelly inside the bread, it tastes awful.

Recruitment

I hear this almost every day: "Brandon, we have got a supply and demand issue. I can't find someone. Not only can I not find healthcare professionals or clinicians, but I am even struggling to find a good receptionist or a good office manager. I want someone like you in a little bottle that I can afford to run my practice."

And I always say, "Well, you have got to find the right person and you have got to have the right systems in place."

So it all starts with finding the candidate. Let's create your recruitment brand. What do you represent you? What do you stand for? Why should a candidate pick you? What's their experience?

Remember we were talking about that Apple experience. Employees act the same way, especially as we target different generations. You have to understand that experience is going to become more important for the employees the younger they get. I've noticed that among the millennial generation, they want an experience—even in the workplace—like nobody else's business. What's your experience and why should they pick you?

The other consideration to remember is what are the employees saying about you, how is it to work for you? Have you ever Googled your company? What comes up? I don't just mean what comes up about the company on Google or on Yelp; what are your employees saying?

Go on glassdoor.com to find the unvarnished truth about what your employees think of you. Look at how they rank you. Look at the communication that is written about you.

It is true that it is a lot more common for an angry person to talk about you than a happy person. But it's so important that you also empower your team to love their employer and employee experience enough to write about it.

What's your job description? What does it look like? I ask this because when I go into clients' practices, they'll often ask me to consult on the recruitment and management of their team. The first thing I tell them is, "Show me your job description."

They'll reply, "Oh, you want me to send the job ad?"

I reply, "No, what's the job description?"

Remember that distinction between public relations and advertising. We want a job description, not an ad. We want something that people can sink their teeth into and consider the qualifications for. What does that look like?

The last consideration to keep in mind about your recruitment brand is what's your differentiation strategy as an employer? Are you throwing in benefits? Is there a true work-life balance? Are you training your employees and providing ongoing mentorship, which is hugely important to workers today. All of these things are important when you're defining your recruitment brand? Once we know your brand and job descriptions, you can better articulate what's amazing about you.

One of the common pieces of feedback that you will hear in the recruiting world from HR is how difficult it is to find quality candidates for positions.

Sourcing has become its own industry. Fifty years ago you had someone who was the office manager that would basically put out a job ad. They would pull in some referrals from their network and interview them. Today you have an entire industry built entirely around sourcing and finding candidates. This isn't limited to ads—the internet and LinkedIn have truly changed the game. There are a number of different avenues to explore here.

Of course, there are the job boards. Over the last five years, Indeed has become the real leader for job boards. Many job boards are actually aggregated from these sites, so they are the true leaders. You may even find your company ending up on mailing lists because of Indeed and their job aggregating software. This can actually be an incredible tool—you used to be fairly limited in your ability to reach certain candidates. You were essentially limited to a defined geographic area. Today you can easily go out and find the very best in the world regardless of where they are located.

The service that I use is called Applicant Pro. It has been an incredible tool for me. I post a job, and it is instantly sent to hundreds of free job boards.

As in every other aspect of the business, social media also remains a big player. Not only the obvious player like LinkedIn—we also heavily leverage sources like Facebook, Pinterest, and Twitter. With all of the contact information readily available on these platforms, you have more incredible pathways to find talent than ever before in history.

Job fairs also remain a major source of finding new talent. I will often make it a point to personally go to college and recent graduate fairs. The return on your time might not be as exponentially big as using social media, but it can be effective to get old fashioned face time in with rising talent.

Word of mouth is another effective outlet. By building a strong relationship with your team and letting them know that you are looking for new staffers to share the journey, you can tap into their individual networks.

This also speaks to the need to create a great employee experience, one that makes your staffers excited about work and excited about recruiting their friends to come along as well.

Many practice owners also simply go old school. The return on investment may be missing, but some of the tools can be effective—post cards, snail mail, etc. My wife who is an occupational therapist gets about a hundred of these inquiries in the mail each month; work for this company, work for that company. She's never called one of them. But if you want to just blast out the word and get your name out, you can definitely do it. I have personally found that the return on investment is lower for something like that.

So now you have sourced some leads. You've got all these leads coming in. They're landing in your lap, and you're overwhelmed. "Brandon, I have 20 interviews!"

Great! Twenty interviews of solid candidates. Now you have to evaluate the candidate. So, I have come up with a special five-step process that has transformed the way that I hire employees.

Are you ready for it?

One—have an application questionnaire.

Sounds simple, but it really works. I get the big questions out of the way. First and foremost if I'm hiring a clinician—are you licensed? You'd be amazed by how many times, I've gotten applicants for positions that they're not even qualified for. That questionnaire will get them right out of the queue so they don't waste my time.

The next thing I want you to do is conduct an email interview. I do this for two reasons. One is that I actually get to ask more questions that I need, including what their desired compensation is. But the most important reason why I do an email communication interview is that I want to see how they write.

I can track how fast they reply and how bad they want that job. I will tell you there are people that wait too long and when they finally email, I say, "Sorry, I already hired someone. When you're off my list." Sometimes I haven't even hired someone, but I want to send a message. Timeliness of communication matters.

I also want to see how they communicate. I teach communication to clinicians and healthcare professionals. I actually show this email interview that I do. You would be surprised with the array of answers that I get.

When it's a one word or two word answer, it feels like a Twitter answer. That is a good indication that they are not my person because I am in the people business. My people invest in their words and utilize them wisely. They don't have to write an entire book like this, but they do need to have the capacity to write messages where I can see some shades of personality. I need to be able to see that they're effective in their communication. During this process, they start to build a relationship with me—and yes, I read every single email. My HR department hasn't even gotten involved yet—you know why? Because I'm in the people business, just like all of us.

I have to give my stamp of approval before I get my HR team to give their stamp of approval. I first invest in understanding the person before I invest in the question of whether they are the right fit for the job. Then I do a phone interview—and again, yes it's me. I do all my own phone interviews. I don't let my team do it because I want to get to know the person. And that's where I connect with them. That's where I get to see if they are a fit for my position. Are we a fit for them? Can they achieve their goals under the umbrella of my program? That is very important. I'm looking for retention. I'm looking for continuity of care. During this initial call, I can begin to gain a clear idea of that.

I can hear them for myself. How do they talk? Do they seem genuinely excited or are they just here for a paycheck? What's their experience, and where do they want to go over the next several years?

At this stage, I finally pass the buck to my HR team to conduct an in-person interview and determine whether we have a shared opinion of the candidate's prospects.

At this stage of the process, they have been through quite a lot. They have grown in their investment to this search, as we have. They have conducted an in-person interview, passed evaluations for communications and personality, and so on. At this stage, it's time to conduct a clinical evaluation where they actually participate in an observation with a clinician so that they can make an informed recommendation to me about the candidate's fitness for the position.

A five step process might seem quite rigorous, but it helps to ensure that we hire the right talent. Making a critical hire is one of the most important decisions that you will ever make as a practice leader. Getting rid of someone who is a wrong fit down the line will be a much more costly and painful process, so we do all that we can to ensure that we get it right from the very beginning and avoid that scenario.

In my evaluation criteria, I want to ensure that they bring strong skills to every facet of communication: written, verbal, body language, clinical experience, clinical exposure, clinical reasoning.

I actually ask them to bring in writing samples of their documentation. It might sound unusual for some of them, but these writing skills are an essential component of the role. I want to see how they're clarifying, and I ask them to do it in a HIPAA-compliant way.

Then I want to know their professional goals—what exactly are they trying to achieve in this world? What do they want to achieve now and over the following five years? What's my role in helping them achieve those goals and how can I invest in them? Turnover creates enormous costs and headaches, so I want to do all that I can to build a long-term relationship between the candidate and my practice. Work retention is very important to me and something I look at closely when I evaluate their CV or their resume. How long are they staying at places?

I'm being honest—I won't do an email interview for someone who has been at five jobs in five years. They're not my person. They might be someone else's person, especially given enormous shifts in the economy and a greater transition to short-term projects for many skilled professionals. Unless they have a cover letter that justifies it, they will likely not be a good fit for my particular practice; I am interested in helping people develop skills so that they can stay and advance over the long-term.

I also take a close look at their personalities. I will actually come out and ask them about their personality: Are you left brain dominant or right brain dominant?

I hire both, but it's good for me as a manager also to know how to work with them. Don't forget that I am essentially evaluating the entire person during the interview process: mind, body, and spirit. I want to understand the "why" of what brought them here. What are their driving forces? Not just for being in this profession, but being here today talking to me, applying for this position.

Fundamentally, the one question that we are both seeking an answer is if this position is the right fit for them.

There is a lot of emotional intelligence that goes into these meetings for both parties. Many candidates will be tempted to say what they think you want to hear, but the questions have a way of cutting through any pretense as the interview goes on. It is important to keep in mind that it should very much be a two-way conversation. They are interviewing *you* just as much as you are interviewing *them*. Talented people have no shortage of opportunities available to them—it is important that they are joining an organization that is the right fit, which affirms the importance of both sides being honest and transparent.

I have a current client for who I am going through this entire recruitment process. They have been amazed with the quality and caliber of hires that I'm making because of each of the steps in this process. You can do this too. It's not rocket science, but it takes intention. It also takes being able to look at things from a whole other lens. Open yourself to asking lots of questions and completing the entire hiring process.

The last consideration I urge you to keep in mind is whether a given candidate would be an appropriate person to be working around your family. I take this very seriously as someone who works closely with my family members. I have two young kids and a wife. I always look at the candidate with them firmly in mind. Would I send my wife to this person for therapy or healthcare services? Would I send my kids to work with this person?

If they're not good enough for my family, they're not good enough for my business—clean and simple. The key to each step here is transparency.

On that phone interview I tell them what I pay, and I make sure it's a fit. I don't want to waste their time; there's no negotiation. This is what I can afford—it either works or it doesn't. If it doesn't work long-term, I actually build out their expectation of when they would get a raise if they would even get a raise because some funding sources lock me in at a set rate.

This level of transparency can make for some occasional uncomfortable conversations, but over time they create authentic relationships. In every email that I send, I usually state upfront that I am approaching our interaction with a bias toward transparency. Don't shy away from tough realities. If you are offering a relatively low reimbursement rate, set that expectation upfront. Put it in the job post, and communicate it via email. Don't shy away from telling the truth because it is far worse for a candidate to fall in love with your practice, only to find out that the pay is too low for them.

I frequently compare recruiting to online dating. I actually met my wife through online dating, ironically enough. I always say that how you present yourself and how you deliver is everything. Anyone who has spent some time in the online dating world has likely had the experience of showing up for dates and discovering that your matches have misrepresented themselves. Perhaps they have used an out-of-date photo or had a wittier friend write their profile. It is always much better in the long run to be honest and transparent upfront.

Let's breakdown that hiring process now.

The first step is that when we want to hire someone, provide an offer letter with fully transparent information. My letter includes the candidate's information, the job description and requirements, compensation—everything. Any additional provisions that I have promised are also reflected in the letter.

This is followed by the very important onboarding process. From the moment they walk in the front door, I want them to feel like they are part of the family. I have a swag bag ready, a water bottle with their names on it, and a personalized business card. The goal is to make them comfortable right away as a part of the team.

I have an employee handbook ready to go that clearly spells out the benefits they will be offered, our policies, procedures, etc.

In the welcome package I offer to new hires, I sometimes even send a letter to their family that effectively says, "Thank you so much for being part of our family. We know that your husband or your wife has joined our team. We want you to know that you and your family are part of our family."

It doesn't end at orientation. We schedule regular check-ins to make sure that the new employee feels supported and things are going well. We might hold these every 30 days for the first couple of months as they are coming on.

What about after all this? They have finally joined the team—now it's time to manage them. If you haven't figured it out yet, I'm all about empowerment. So, how we say things is everything. Our words have meaning. If someone's doing something wrong, I don't come in and say, "Josh, you messed up." Instead I approach it more along the lines of, "Josh, can I talk to you for a minute? Let's look at how we can be more effective with this process. Would it be challenging for you to do it this way? Have you ever looked at it from this perspective?"

My goal is to empower my team and inspire them to want to continually improve. Bring them up, enlighten them, take the fear off them, and hold them accountable but make them want to be better through empowerment.

It is crucial to truly understand your team. Understand their personality, understand their professional goals, understand their work ethic, and understand their innate behavior versus learned behavior.

There is no single approach that works for everyone. Every person responds differently. Think of yourself almost as like a coach or a team. When a team wins a Super Bowl, you don't know how much work came from that coaching staff. How do you bring the best out of them? What's their level of buy-in? Different people respond differently to correction. I always recommend that you coach them both from an in-person standpoint and also through a written paper trail. This documentation will give you something to point to so you can remain empowering. Most importantly, having a written paper trail allows you to give specific and clear feedback based on facts, such as—"Do you remember when we had this meeting three weeks ago? Tell me what's going on? Why isn't this working? How can we support you to do better?"

Give them responsibility, hold them accountable, but take a little bit of responsibility too. This is a partnership. After all, it takes two to tango. All of this will help to foster greater employee accountability over time. I even have employees sign an accountability agreement during orientation that helps ensure that we are on the same page when it comes to expectations.

I make sure to clearly show them the metrics they are being evaluated with and ensure that they understand how they are being assessed. If bringing in new clients is a meaningful metric, I want them to fully understand what success looks like.

I strive to make the entire process fun. Few things will motivate your staff as much as creative compensation that sets up clear incentives for their productivity. Perhaps we increase contributions to a shared reward each time a team hits a certain growth goal, for example. This helps to build greater buy-in and provides them a clear goal to strive for.

Take the time to recognize a job well done. An acknowledgement program can ensure that your employees feel valued and recognized for their contributions. Consider giving awards or setting up a regular forum to recognize achievers.

Ultimately your practice's success comes down to organizational culture. Life is too short to be miserable at work. If the stakes are life and death each and every day, your people are going to become so stressed that efficiency will plummet.

We want highly energetic, motivated, and efficient people working together to win the game. Get their buy-in, provide clear incentives, and turn it into a game.

None of this happens overnight. It takes time to learn how to effectively manage your people, in addition to everything else on your plate. But by trusting, empowering, and rewarding your team, you can build a high-functioning culture that needs less and less of your attention over time.

CHAPTER 10

Surviving and Thriving - Implementation Time

"The world is moving so fast that the person who says it can't be done is generally interrupted by someone doing it."
—Elbert Hubbard

All of the work and planning that we have considered throughout this book is important. I hope that you have found value in learning from my own experiences, even though the particulars at your own practice may vary. However, I stress that you should not get too wrapped up in analyzing and strategizing your idea to death. The most important thing to do in any business environment is to get moving on actually implementing your idea.

Look at how rapidly the world has changed in recent years. Today the life expectancy of a company on the S&P has plummeted to around 20 years. Just look at all the disrupters and fast movers coming onto the scene. We are seeing the launch of completely new business models—the world's largest transportation company Uber owns no cars and the world's most valuable hospitality enterprise Airbnb owns no hotels. We are clearly in a new paradigm here. So while there is much to learn from the experiences of those who have come before you, you must also embrace new ideas of your own.

We have nearly made it to the end. We have studied many ideas and covered a lot of territory. That can only mean that the time is approaching to begin implementing these approaches.

I would challenge you to go back through the book and pull out one concept from each chapter to focus on implementing. I know that it can be overwhelming to consider everything that you need to get done to make your practice a success. I suggest making your task easier by breaking it down one chapter at a time, one idea at a time.

Implement one thing from each chapter, and I assure you your practice will reach all your goals and milestones, and you will be sending me "thank you" cards!

We've defined the dream, we defined your business model, and we talked about your workforce…so now what? Let's get the implementation going if you haven't already! Keep in mind some of these steps and consider what you need to tackle next.

Business Steps:

- Lawyer or CPA/Accountant (articles of incorporation, sole proprietorship, copyright, etc.)

- Determine Protective Insurance Requirements (protective insurance) – (liability insurances, worker's compensation insurance, D&O insurance, EPLI insurance, property insurance, etc.

Additional Implementation Steps to Keep in Mind:

- Business Permits / Licensure Steps:

- Business Licensure

- EIN Number (Employer Identification Number)

- NPI Number (If Applicable)

- Home occupation permit (If Applicable)

- Zoning permit (If Applicable)

- Building permit (If Applicable)

- Health department permit (If Applicable)

- Sales tax license (If Applicable)

- Sellers permit (If Applicable)

- Fire and police department permit (If Applicable)

- Withholding tax registration

Financial Steps:

- Payroll Setup

- Accounts Payable / Accounts Receivable Structure— Software, personnel, etc.

- Bank Accounts (Checking and Savings Accounts)

- Funding / SBA Application or Self-Funded?

Contracting Steps:

- Submit RFPs (Request for Proposal) for state or federal funded services

- Contact Insurance Companies & Third Party Insurance Networks to Contract (If Applicable)

- Medicare / Medicaid Contracts

- Worker's Compensation Contracts

- Staffing Contracts (SNF, Home Health, School, etc.)

- Determine Cash Pay Fee Schedule / Contracts, etc.

Additional Operations/Implementation Steps to Keep in Mind:

- Operations Coordination:

- Identify Location(s)—(as applicable)

- Identify Staffing Needs With 12-month projections and timeline

- Employee Handbook

- OSHA paperwork (Occupational Safety and Health Administration) / Injury and Illness Prevention Program

- Benefits Administration (if applicable)—healthcare, 401k, etc.

- Equipment (Computers, Therapy equipment, testing materials, tools, etc.)

- Documentation, Scheduling and Billing Technology (EMR, Clearinghouses, outsource, etc.)

- CPT/ICD—10 Resources (if doing insurance)

- Invoicing Templates (If Applicable)

- Credit Card Processing (If Applicable)

- Reminder Patient Call/Text Service (If Applicable)

- Accounting Software (QuickBooks, etc.)

- Compliance for consumers (HIPAA forms, policy and procedure manual, consumer paperwork, intake paperwork, etc.)

- Organization Board (Document Functions, Systems, Statistics)

- Communication Systems (Phone, Fax, Email, etc.)

Marketing / Branding Steps:

- Brand Development

- Practice Name

- Logo(s)

- Slogans / Brand Identifiers

- Website

- Social Media

- Business Cards

- Business Emails

- Letterhead

- Brochures

- Postcards

- Flyers

Business Development Steps:

- Referral Database

- Build Database of referral sources

- Build Database of potential client sources

- Build Database of Referral Networking Opportunities (Events, Meetups, SAGE, etc.)

- Market Strategy and Forecasting

- Budget for Marketing

- Implementation Timeline

- Roll Out Of Marketing Initiatives

- Introduction Letter

- Marketing Statistics Spreadsheet

- Start Setting

Clinical Setup / Structure:

- Documentation Templates (Daily Notes, Progress Reports, etc.)

- Documentation Stable Datums Based on Funding Source

- Authorization of Services Systems (As Applicable)

- Clinical Education / Continuing Education (As Applicable)

- Senior Clinical Leadership / Outcome Monitoring (As Applicable)

There's a lot to do! But don't be overwhelmed. Take your time as you work through the list.

First and foremost, do be sure to talk to a lawyer or a CPA. I think you need that advice, and I think it's worth the investment. There are things that we do in life that are worth the investment—this surely is one of them. Anyone can file your paperwork but really delve into the details of if you should be an LLC, an S Corp, a C Corp, or whatever you may choose. This is an area where speaking with an expert can help enormously.

The next thing I want you to pay especially close attention to is determining the protective insurance requirements that you need. This means your liability insurance, workers compensation, directors and officers insurance, property insurance, and so on. You may likely not need all of them, but you likely will need some of them. Meeting with an advisor and breaking down your needs will help to clarify what can be a very confusing area of the business.

Take time to sort out your business permits and license. You don't want to make any mistakes here. If you're serving food or coffee at your business, for example, that can have a big impact on the zoning and building permits that are appropriate for you.

You will also need to invest time in setting up your financial foundation. Do you have a payroll company? How are you cutting your checks? Who is handling your accounts payable? What's the structure? How are you doing your deposits? How are you cutting checks? Do you have a major bank that you're working with? These are all things you want to be clear on.

Funding is another important consideration. Are you going to go get loans? Are you going to go get angel investors? Are you going to go get a loan from the Small Business Administration? These are all things that you want to start looking at.

Operations will be a critical part of your job—identifying the right location for your business, identifying staffing needs, setting up a human resources system. If you feel yourself overwhelmed, refer back to your employee handbook that you have developed and work with experts to make sure you are compliant with all regulations. You are not alone, and I am here if I can ever be of support to you in any way. From online webinars to digital courses to consultations to even management services, I am passionate about supporting your entrepreneurial goals in any way I can.

Secrets to Managing a Successful Practice

Take it one step at a time. And remember a few key secrets for managing a successful private practice. The first is to carefully think through your strategy before making major changes. You just spent 10 chapters learning the nuts and bolts—let's get those strategies ironed out.

As I have said before, business is much more enjoyable if you can make it a game. Tie outcomes for your employees to bonus structures—in the same way that you might make points the rewards in a video game—and you will be amazed at what they can achieve. Give your team buy-in, compensate them creatively and generously, and give them enough rope to explore what they can do on their own.

Keep in mind the importance of adequate cash flow. Prove yourself through cash flow analysis and make sure that your systems are in place. Invest in efficiency and you have my word that it will save big dollars for your practice, allowing you to scale faster.

Implement a measure twice, cut once mentality with all that you do. One step in front of another and there's nothing you can't achieve.

In all your zeal to succeed, don't cut corners and don't ignore ethics. I just heard the other day about a practice on the East Coast where the owner was arrested and placed in jail for fraud. You didn't get into this industry for that. (She likely did not either, but it is easy to get caught up in taking shortcuts when cash is flowing in.) Provide ethical treatment, provide value. Be a puzzle piece player versus taking a short and easy route that ends in closure. Always be improving.

This is a hustle. Get ready for it. If you weren't born to hustle, you're in the wrong space. You aren't born an entrepreneur; you need to invest in these skills just as you have throughout your career. It takes hustle and efficiency to get to the finish line.

My motto is to always work smarter, not harder. This can be a hard concept for many of us who are health professionals. We are used to tackling our problems with sheer willpower and putting in insane hours, pulling all-nighters when necessary. This is a recipe for surefire burnout when launching your own business. You need to know your strengths and delegate to people that you trust.

Know when to call a favor in, know when to hire help, bring in strategic initiatives outside of your control to give you advice. As I have written, I believe this is a relationship-based business. There is no need to tackle all of your challenges alone; in fact, you will go much farther if you have the humility to ask for help.

Hopefully this won't apply to you, but know when to cut your losses. I have killed businesses before. I've been there. I've seen when a business simply wasn't working out; there wasn't enough upside. Don't be afraid to cut your losses. Know when to call a spade a spade and get out. You can chalk up any failures to a learning experience. When you need to change directions, it's a sign of strength, not weakness. So make that change and pivot, pivot, pivot.

FINAL THOUGHTS

I want you to hear me loud and clear—you *can* do this.

You got it. It's in you. You wouldn't be reading this book if it wasn't in you. Identify your strengths and weaknesses. If you need help, there's help here. There are people in our community that are here to support your dream. Find an accountability advisor and build a team. Don't do this alone.

Write out your vision; write down a positive mantra that pushes you to be at your best every day. Remember the Stuart Smalley character from *Saturday Night Live*? As he always said, "I am good enough, I am smart enough, and gosh darn it people like me."

It's not a bad mantra! What's yours? Have your mantra! I know it sounds funny, but it's important. Paint your ideal scene of what success looks like and look at it every day. When I was growing up my dad used to have this picture of a Porsche. I said, "Dad, why is that on your wall? You love Porsches?"

He said, "I will own this one day."

That gave him motivation. Different people have different motivation. For you, it might be a car or financial freedom or more time to spend with your loved ones. It might be a mission—a stronger and more humane healthcare system. Whether your goal is changing the world or building greater financial independence (or both), conjure a clear vision of what victory looks like.

We are fortunate to be working in one of the single most exciting industries in the world—and likely the most important. We don't all necessarily need technology or finance depending on how we organize our lives, but all of us depend on quality healthcare. At some point, all of us interact with the healthcare system, which we can all agree could stand for major reform and innovation. As big as the challenges in the current system are, there are also enormous opportunities to be seized. I hope that you are as excited each day as I am to go to work to hopefully make the system function better and improve the quality of life for all of those who walk through our doors.

And don't do it alone. None of us can succeed entirely alone. I can't tell you all of the hundreds of people that help me every day, simply as I reflect on what I have learned from each of them. That part of the journey never really ends. I am always learning. I am always asking for help and growing each day. That is what keeps me excited and motivated each day.

I wish the same for you. I wish you an exciting journey in which you embrace change, set high goals, and pass on your success to others.

Let's get to work!